MAKING TIME, MAKING MONEY

Making Time, Making Money

A Step-by-Step Program
for Setting Your Goals
and Achieving Success

by RITA DAVENPORT

ST. MARTIN'S PRESS·NEW YORK

To my mother and father, sister and brother, whose love gave me strength; to my husband, whose love gave me support; to my sons Michael and Scott, whose love made me complete.

Library of Congress Cataloging in Publication Data

Davenport, Rita.
    Making time, making money.

    1. Success. 2. Business. 3. Time management.
I. Title.
HP5386.D215   650.1   81-21492
ISBN 0-312-50801-8   AACR2
ISBN 0-312-50802-6 (pbk.)

Design by Mina Greenstein

10   9   8   7

Contents

Introduction
Time Management
Can Make You a
Winner

Would you like to be a winner? The desires that have always sparked your dreams—playing Beethoven's Moonlight Sonata, owning a wardrobe of beautiful designer originals, starring in a Broadway play, living in a mansion, driving a Ferrari—can be achieved.

Perhaps your dreams are less glamorous. Maybe you would just like to smile when your child spills chocolate syrup on your newly washed kitchen floor, or finish that quilt you started making three years ago.

Although everyone defines the specifics a little differently, winning really means getting what you want out of life. It means spending time the way you want to spend it. It means creating a life-style that suits your needs and interests.

By my own definition I am a winner. I am not a millionaire and I haven't climbed Mount Everest or run a twenty-six-mile marathon, but I do spend my time doing the things that bring me the greatest joy and satisfaction. This book is designed to help you achieve the same kind of success in your own life.

Unfortunately, many of us are like the woman who saved her money for ten years so she could take a European cruise. When the day arrived to pay for her fare she reasoned, "I have just enough money for the tickets. To enjoy the ship's meals would be too expensive. So, I shall take a large supply of cheese and crackers."

While on board the lady eagerly participated in all planned activities, but when mealtimes came she quietly slipped into her room to munch on her scanty fare. Finally the long voyage was about to end. The woman decided to splurge and eat with the rest of the passengers in the dining room. After enjoying the feast she asked for the check.

The waiter responded, "Oh, there is no check, madame. You purchased your meals when you purchased your ticket."

Like that woman, many of us fail accurately to read our ticket for life. We assume happiness and fulfillment can only come to others. We sup on meals of cheese and crackers, telling ourselves we don't have enough money, we don't have the time, or that there are too many demands on us already. You might even be telling yourself, "I don't have the talent or resources to get what I really want out of life." Remember, we each have the same amount of time. No one is given more than twenty-four hours a day, and no one is given less.

William James, the nineteenth-century philosopher, wrote, "Compared to what we ought to be, we are only half awake. Our fires are dampened, our drafts are checked. We are making use of only a small part of our mental and physical resources."

I invite you to come to the banquet table. Life can be enjoyed to the fullest. You can unlock the door of your great potential. It all starts with a belief in yourself, a road map, and some principles of time management.

Along with the information and time-saving tips in this book, you will find your own personal workbook section with assignments for you to complete. In fact, you will be enjoying the same experience as you would if you had participated in one of my time-management workshops. The concepts in this book can change your life. But remember, it all starts and ends with you and the way you choose to use your time. Good luck, and may you make all your dreams come true.

1

Winning Is a Matter
of Choice

*Most of us go through life not knowing what we
want, but feeling darned sure this isn't it.*
                              —The Cosmic Humorist

Before you begin reading this book, I want you to stop for a moment and become totally aware of your here and now. Take your mind out of the past and the future and focus on the present moment. Breathe deeply, close your eyes, and then take a good hard look at yourself, inside and out. Observe your surroundings too. Did you know that everything you are experiencing at this very moment is the result of your choices?

Think about it. You are in control right now, and your circumstances—physical, mental, spiritual, social, emotional, financial, and environmental—are a result of the hundreds and thousands of choices you have made throughout your lifetime. The choices you make from this moment onward will determine who and what you are tomorrow, next month, a year from now, five years from now, and so on. We are ultimately responsible for our own success, our personal happiness, and our relationships with others. And that can be a pretty scary realization if you've been putting the responsibility elsewhere.

4

"Ah," you may say, "but I can't be responsible for everything. After all, lots of things that have affected my life I didn't choose at all. I don't plan everything that happens and so I can't be totally responsible!"

You're right of course. You can't control *all* of the events that affect your life, but you can decide *how* they will affect it. Let me give you an example.

I grew up with a young man who was told that because he wasn't really smart he was going to have to work twice as hard if he was ever going to have anything. Now I can think of a lot of people who would be crushed if they heard those words and feel very inferior because of them. But this young man took the advice about the hard work and forgot about the rest. As a result, he now has a chain of businesses, lives in a beautiful, affluent neighborhood, and is enjoying a great deal of financial success.

Accepting responsibility for our lives can seem awesome at first, but it can also be pretty exciting. After all, who cares more about you than you? Time and choice. That's all any of us have, but the way you use them will bring ultimate joy or continual frustration.

RIDE A HORSE IN THE DIRECTION IT'S GOING!

A few years ago a friend of mine earned a quarter of a million dollars in one year. I was proud of her—not jealous, for I'd gotten over that time-waster long ago—and was curious to know why she was so much more productive than I. (By the way, you suffer if you resent your friends' accomplishments. Unless someone takes from you to prosper it is only to your advantage to have successful friends. No one benefits from associating with losers!)

Anyway, my curiosity caused me to quiz her about her

abilities. I guess I really wanted to know whether she was smarter than I. She admitted that in college her overall grade average had only been fair. She had barely made it into graduate school. I, on the other hand, had always been proud of my excellent grades, so I knew she was no smarter than I—at least not academically.

Still I was curious. I knew nothing about astrology but wondered whether she had been born under a lucky sign—I found out we were born on the very same day! So much for luck, which I never believed in anyway. I now know that the harder we work, the luckier we get.

Well, I knew she worked hard, but then so did I. So what was the reason for the difference in our productivity? When I finally asked her the secret of her success, I found she had learned to ride a horse in the direction it was going. That wasn't what she said, but it was how I interpreted her explanation. Let me clarify.

She decided to evaluate what she was capable of doing and focus on that ability. She concentrated her efforts in one direction. She became a specialist at something and made it profitable. Next, she decided to take a course from Dr. Charles Hobbs, a specialist in time management. He taught her how to focus her energy, concentrate her power, and set her priorities.

JUST IN TIME

I immediately began to focus on time management as the missing ingredient necessary to my own success. For years I had given lip service to inspirational ideas as a motivational speaker, but was never really that successful myself. I decided to find out everything I possibly could about successful time management. I started with Dr. Hobbs's course and then made a master list of thirty-eight daydreams or objectives. At the top of that list was the goal to become the number one woman in the field of time management. In order to accomplish that goal I decided to do something every single day to improve my abilities to use my time more effectively or help someone else in that task. Writing this book and sharing my learnings with you is the culmination of that goal.

HOW MOTIVATED ARE YOU TO BECOME YOUR BEST SELF?

I want you to think for a moment and then ask yourself these questions:

1. Do you really believe you deserve to get what you want in life?
2. Do you deserve to free that special genius within you—all of those gifts and talents that can enrich your life and the lives of others?
3. Do you deserve to be happy?
4. Do you see yourself as being just as worthy and lovable as anyone else?
5. Do you constantly measure yourself as inferior or superior to others, or do you see all people as separate and unique, trying to make it through this human condition together?
6. If you knew you could not fail, how would you choose to earn a living?

Time management, as you will find in reading this book, is one of the most important keys to your success. But it is only a key. Before you can use that key you have to be motivated; and before that can happen, you have to find out what a terrific and wonderful person you really are.

MEASURING YOUR SELF-ESTEEM

Self-esteem is an emotion. It is how a person feels about him-or herself, on the basis of an individual sense of worth and importance. It has to do with our individual awareness and includes everything we perceive through our five senses and all of our intuitions. It is a result of our total conditioning, our life experiences, our innate intelligence, our insights, urges, emotional reactions, and every decision we make. Unfortunately, many of us have experiences in life that limit or distort our awareness. Let's consider a few of these:

Our Parents

In any case we should be grateful to our parents for the gift of life itself and for all of the positive things our heritage has given us. We should also be grateful for the many sacrifices they have made for our benefit. But we should also be aware of a possible curse that may have been handed down with that heritage—the curse of low self-esteem. Unfortunately, a large percentage of our population suffers from such a curse. You must realize that if your parents in any way gave you a message that made you feel not as good as or less lovable than others, they were wrong—absolutely and completely wrong! Often the messages we get are so subtle and are given in so many ways that it becomes difficult not to buy it. But the reality is that you are wonderful. You are special. There is no one more deserving than you!

Other People

Sadly, many people grow up, get married—or don't get married—surrounded by people who give negative, "you're-not-okay" messages. Some of us are married to people who give us these messages. Some of us have friends who give us these messages, and some of us are locked into jobs where there is a constant barrage of "you're-not-okay-ness." Unfortunately, many of us buy these messages.

The fact is, when a person gives you a negative message, he is holding up a distorted mirror. You have to start looking into another mirror—the mirror that lies within yourself. It's the only one that can show you what your special qualities are, and it is only when we look within that we begin to love ourselves.

A close relative of mine has suffered from poor self-esteem her whole life because her grades in school were compared to those of her friends in the neighborhood who were more academically inclined. It was unfair that she had to compete with other people rather than herself. She felt intimidated when they made good grades, and she felt she deserved to be looked down upon. And yet this woman is one of the most kind, generous, sensitive, and loving people I know. But she doesn't want to acknowledge those things. She prefers to remain in a mental environment that makes her feel inferior.

Procrastination and Lack of Self-discipline

Another way we affect our self-esteem is by making unwise decisions. On a regular basis we choose to take the worst-self road or the road of least resistance instead of doing those things that would make us happy and successful.

I'd like you to imagine yourself on a road. As you walk along this very beautiful path, you come to a sudden detour. You have to make a choice to go one way or the other. You can't stand still and you can't avoid the choice. Now think of that detour as a possible temptation. If you're on a diet, it may be a piece of pie that has been offered to you. If you're trying to control your temper, it may be a provocation that could cause you to lose it. It would be so easy to turn onto the side road. You've made that decision many times before. But the problem is, once we're on that road, it's pretty hard to get off it. The only thing it offers is unhappiness, but still we make those choices. Every time we make such a choice we lower our self-esteem. Only by consistently making the choice that is truly best for us can we raise our self-esteem and maintain it.

Repeated Defeats and Failures

Everyone has failures some of the time, and some of us have failures a lot of the time. How we react to those failures can have a grave affect on our self-esteem. A lot of that reaction is determined by how much value we place on the thing we failed at. If a man's total sense of self-worth is based on his ability to hold a particular job, then losing that job may have a completely destructive effect on his self-esteem. Or if a woman's sense of self-worth is based on her ability to love and be loved by a particular man and that man chooses to stop loving her, she can feel utterly destroyed in the process.

We have to learn to disassociate ourselves from our failures, and that is not an easy thing to do, particularly if winning and achieving are important to us. But since no one is perfect, we're all going to fail some of the time. If we choose to make those losses learning experiences we will ultimately benefit and become successful in our endeavors, but if we choose to berate ourselves endlessly, we will lower our self-esteem more and more, until we have ultimately put ourselves in a place where it is almost impossible to be happy or successful.

BUILDING OUR SELF-ESTEEM

Fortunately, no one has to perpetuate low self-esteem. We can rediscover that special spark within each of us, begin to visualize it, and then transform it into actions. As we do so, our self-esteem will go upward and so will our happiness, our productivity, and our motivation.

At this point in my life I can honestly say I feel pretty terrific about myself. But that wasn't always the case. I can still remember how envious I was of another little girl in my grade-school class. She seemed to have everything: she was cute, popular, talented, and best of all, she got to take dancing lessons. I remember feeling jealous during "hobby week" when she displayed her ballet shoes and costumes.

Today that woman and I are very good friends. She's still outstanding and special in every way, but I no longer feel inferior. I feel very worthy of our friendship because I now realize I have my own gifts and abilities.

How We Feel What We Feel

Since one's self-esteem is a feeling rather than an intellectual inventory of personal assets and liabilities, it is important to know how we trigger those feelings. You will find that page 205 of your workbook is entitled "How I Feel What I Feel." For the next week, jot down every time you feel inferior or "less than" and the circumstances that made you feel that way.

Let me give you an illustration. A friend of mine recently broke up with a man she loved dearly and had hoped to marry. Breaking up was hard enough, but dealing with her replacement was even worse. Her replacement was a beautiful blonde woman who had been the homecoming queen and a cheerleader at the university she had attended. My friend said she had vivid recollections of how pretty and popular this girl had been in college, and she immediately felt intimidated and put down.

Admittedly, dealing with a replacement who is reputed to be very beautiful and to have all of those status honors can be pretty rough. But it's still a matter of self-esteem. The only reason my friend didn't try out for those things in college was because she felt as if she weren't worthy. In reality, she had every quality necessary to achieve those honors then or to have whatever she might want now.

Overcoming Procrastination

Every time you procrastinate—avoid something you know you should be doing—you lower your self-esteem. On page 206 of your workbook you can list everything you have been procrastinating about. They may be big things or little things, but whatever they are, write them down. I challenge you to start working on that list today. Remember the statement, "If not now, when? If not by me, by whom?" I promise you that as you attack the items on that list, your self-esteem will begin to rise.

Overcoming Guilt, Forgiving, and Removing Bad Feelings

Feeling guilt is an absolute waste of time unless there is something you can do to change the situation. If you have been dishonest, by all means you should feel guilty, because that guilt will motivate you to ask for forgiveness. But if you are feeling guilt over a situation that is now past—if indeed there is nothing you can now do to change the situation—then you've got to stop feeling bad and get on with life. The same applies to forgiving others. How much time and energy do you waste by failing to forgive and forget? On page 207 of your workbook, you will see three sections: "Guilt I feel over situations that cannot be changed"; "Guilt I feel because of wrongs I have failed to right"; and "People I am angry with or feeling hurt or wronged by." In the first section, write it all down, get it out of your system, and then do everything you can to forget it. Above all, stop blaming yourself. In the second section take action. If you need to apologize, apologize. If you need to correct a wrong, correct a wrong. If you need to ask forgiveness from the Lord, then ask forgiveness; don't let it hang—it will rob you of your energy, your enthusiasm, and your good feelings about yourself. In the third section, I want you to think seriously of the ways you can stop feeling angry or hurt by others. Imagine how you would feel if you were in the other person's shoes. How would you want to be treated? It's not always easy to forgive another individual overnight, but you can begin taking positive steps toward that end. As you do, your own feelings of self-esteem will grow.

VISUALIZATION

Flip Wilson's character Geraldine says, "What you see is what you get." Little does Geraldine know the importance of what she is saying. Everything we are and are not at this moment is the result of our thinking—conscious or subconscious. It is the way we get our level of self-esteem. If we want to raise our self-esteem, we must change our self-image. We can do this by visualization.

Ninety percent of us think in pictures. If you're uncertain as to whether you can visualize or not, try this simple test: think of a beautiful rose. Imagine its color and texture and even its scent. If you can see that rose in your mind without going out to the garden to look at one, you can visualize.

It has also been said that ninety-five percent of our actions and reactions are subconsciously motivated. In other words, the majority of things we do on a day-to-day basis are the result of our past thinking. Most of this programming takes place when we are infants. In fact, some educators and social scientists have estimated that a child in his first few years of life may learn up to twenty-five times as much every day as an adult does. That is why it is so vitally important to program our children with positive images of themselves.

My friend Dolly Parton (who, by the way, married one of my old high school friends) started programming herself from a very early age to be successful. When she was only seven years old, the fourth in a family of twelve children, she decided she wanted to be a star—"the biggest in the world." She wanted pretty clothes and attention and to buy things for Mama and Daddy. She admitted to having heartaches and disappointments, but she never let them block her vision of the future.

If you want to think differently about yourself, if you want to look and act differently, you must begin to visualize yourself in new ways. The Old Testament teaches us that "As [a man] thinketh in his heart, so is he." (Proverbs 23:7)

One of the most powerful examples of positive visualization working to change a person's reality is described by Dr. Carl Simonton, who has successfully used visualization to facilitate the healing of cancer patients. For those patients who have an intense desire to live, Dr. Simonton and his staff get the patient to visualize a force working within themselves to rid the body of bad cancer cells. It is left up to the cancer patient to use whatever force he or she chooses. Some individuals visualize chemicals or medicines dissolving their bad cancer cells. Others pick animals such as dogs or man-eating fish to eat away that which is harmful to their systems. It's all visualization, but it works. The body often heals itself and becomes well.

Treasure Mapping

Visualization is most successful when all five senses are used. This method is often called "treasure mapping." You begin the process by looking through magazines or finding pictures from other sources that describe in vivid detail what you want to look like, feel like, or what you want to accomplish. Next, you take active steps positively to stimulate your other senses toward believing in this goal. For example, if you want a new 280 Mercedes sportscar, I would suggest you go to the dealer and get a picture of the exact car you would like to own. While you're visiting the showroom, go for a test drive. As you sit in the car, feel the genuine leather, smell the newness of the auto, and remember what it feels like to drive it. Visualize yourself driving that car every day. Then visualize yourself earning the money to purchase it.

Where to Start Picturing

Everyone needs a place where they can think without interruption, to visualize, to meditate, to pray, and to plan. I want you to find a place where you can do that. Some of my friends are able to go into meditative states when they jog. For me, it's the bathroom. I can lock the door, sit down on the floor, and spread out my plans for the day. I can also review my overall objectives, relax, close my eyes, and visualize the things I'm trying to accomplish. I use visualization every day and I believe in it one hundred percent. It's one of the best ways that I know of to raise self-esteem and level of awareness.

AFFIRMATIONS

We all talk to ourselves every day. The key is to become aware of that inner dialogue and start programming it to raise your self-esteem and help you to have the internal desire to become more successful. We can do this by giving ourselves positive affirmations. Here's how it works.

On page 208, you will find a place to list positive, present-centered statements such as, "I do first things first," or "I have terrific enthusiasm about being alive today!" After you repeat the affirmation, take a deep breath, visualize yourself making the affirmation a reality, and then do it. I don't mean do it tomorrow or next week or even in an hour. Do it that moment. Affirmations only work when they lead to a positive action. They work best when the action is practiced directly after reading the affirmation.

Besides writing your affirmations on cards, I highly recommend a magazine called *Science of the Mind,* published by United Church of Religious Science, P.O. Box 75127, Los Angeles, California 90075. It offers an affirmation for every day of the month. If read and practiced, these affirmations can have a very beneficial effect, even on the subconscious level.

IT'S ALL UP TO YOU

I remember when I was in the third grade I tried to win a bicycle, the grand prize in a contest at Garrett Drug Store. I tried, but someone else tried a little harder. I didn't get the grand prize—only first runner-up—and that prize was a useless toy sewing machine.

For years I kicked myself, not because I was too lazy to put out the effort to win but because I ended up with a used bicycle, which was all my folks could afford.

I've only recently realized how wise my parents were. Had they compensated for my disappointment in losing with a new bike, I'd never have learned a great lesson: you get what you deserve. I had made the choices to get that toy sewing machine instead of the new bike. I don't make that mistake any more. I want the best in life and intend to pay the prices necessary to enjoy it. Remember you must pay a price for everything you receive. I offer you the same opportunity. You deserve the best too!

2
Success—How to Be a Who's Who Instead of a Who's That

Do you feel like a winner? Are you happy with the way you are
currently spending your time? Think about it. Are you really getting what you want out of life? Are you achieving your goals?
Do you spend time on your most important priorities or waste
it on trivia? Do you even know what it takes to make you feel
happy?

Emerson said, "The crowning fortune of a man is to be born
to some pursuit which finds his employment and happiness,
whether it be to make baskets, or broad swords, or canals, or
statues, or songs."

I agree with Emerson. There is a direct correlation between
our internal happiness and the way we choose to spend our time.
In this chapter we are going to be taking an in-depth look at
the way you currently spend time and then determine what it
will take to make you happy and satisfied with your life.

WHERE DOES YOUR TIME GO?

I am going to give you a tough assignment now. It's difficult because it requires great self-discipline, but it really is the only way to find out what is happening with your time and your emotional relationship to it.

For the next week I want you to measure and study your schedule of actions and events from five different perspectives:

1. **Action taken.** Write down everything you do with your time. You might want to make a notation every half hour or every hour, but list all activities as specifically as possible.

2. **Time spent.** As you complete each small chore or large project, indicate how long it took to finish the task. For example, did it take you fifteen minutes to clean the oven or a half hour? How long did it take you to work up that presentation for your boss or make out the menus for the week? You may want to use a timer or a stopwatch for accuracy.

3. **Purpose or objective.** Before beginning each activity, indicate the purpose or objective. If, for example, you choose to call a friend at five o'clock, what will you hope to accomplish? Do you want to relay information or do you want to let her know you have been thinking about her? Maybe you know she's been down and you want to cheer her up. Or perhaps you are making the call simply to avoid accomplishing a more important but more difficult task.

4. **Results.** Critique your work or activity. Did you accomplish what you set out to achieve? Were you happy with the results? Could you have done it better? How long did it take? Were the results worth it? Did you reap any rewards?

5. **Emotional response.** This is probably one of the most important categories. Describe how you felt about each activity. Did you enjoy the way you spent your time or did you detest it? Were you resentful of interruptions? Was it easy to become totally involved in your work or did you find your mind wandering? If you could have been doing anything with your

time at that particular moment, would you have selected another activity?

Record your findings in a notebook for one week. At the end of the week use the following questions to evaluate your activities:

1. What were your most significant accomplishments? What did you accomplish during the week? Would you consider your productivity level high or low? If you were unhappy about your performance level, consider the reasons that contributed to this. Could some items easily have been changed?

2. How many activities were enjoyable to you? During the week, how many times were you able to write "I enjoyed what I was doing"; "I felt a real sense of accomplishment"; "Even though it was tough, I'm glad I stuck it out"?

One sure way to determine your level of enjoyment from a task is to analyze your level of personal involvement. Recently I read of a writer who could literally spend hours at a time totally involved in his work. He could lose all sense of what was going on around him because of his deep enthusiasm for the project. I've heard of similar experiences from professional athletes and musicians. But you don't have to be an athlete or an artist to experience this kind of high. I know of a man who is a top salesman. He believes in his product and he enjoys talking with people. He reaches a real peak or high when he's making a sales pitch or closing a deal. A friend of mine went into modeling because she said it was the one place where her mind didn't wander. Being in front of a camera and working with a photographer was a totally captivating experience for her.

3. How often were you bored or unhappy? As you look over your time log, are there many places where you wrote "I hate what I'm doing"; "I am totally dissatisfied"; "I'm working, but I'm daydreaming about something else"; "I feel uncomfortable in this situation"?

Granted, not everyone can have highs twenty-four hours a day, but if you find yourself involved in work or tasks that continually drain you and leave you with no sense of satisfaction, you are probably spending your time doing the wrong things.

4. **If you continue as you have for the past week, where will you be in five years?** If you continue with the same job, the same activities, the same habits, and the same level of achievement, where will you be in five years—physically, economically, socially, emotionally, and spiritually? More important, will you be happy with your lot in life?

PLANNING FOR THE FUTURE

Greg Daneke, a highly respected consultant to big business and government on natural resource planning, has explained, "Planning is not forecasting or predicting the future; rather, it is the creation of the future." That is what time management is all about—planning to use your time in a way that will bring you the greatest satisfaction and personal rewards.

There are several ways of determining what you need to be happy and successful in life. You can take an aptitude test or talk with a career counselor, but sometimes that can be misleading. In my workshops I have found seven key exercises to be most effective. After completing them, many clients have made career changes and eliminated time-wasting or nonproductive activities. Others have taken steps to spend more time with their spouses and children. And still others have taken unique risks. They have gone on adventures, experienced life in new and different ways, expanded their circle of friends, and on the whole become happier, more fulfilled people. I promise that the same kinds of positive results can occur in your life.

Exercise 1: Favorite Ways to Spend Your Time

I am often amazed at how few people take time to think about the activities which bring them the most pleasure and satisfaction.

Recently, a very successful and happy man was counseling a group of college students. He said, "If I could give you one piece of advice, it would be to find a way to make money doing the things you enjoy the most in life. If you do this, every day will be like a holiday. But if you rely on a two-week vacation once a year to find happiness, you will be miserable."

On page 209 of your workbook section you will find a chart. There is space to list twenty of your favorite activities. After you have finished the exercise, analyze your findings. Did any of the items surprise you? Did any of the items correlate with your current employment or activities? Were there any items listed that could be turned into career success?

One homemaker who completed the assignment placed reading at the top of her favorite-activities list. She had been hoping to find a way of bringing in an extra income; now she has a "story-time" hour at the local library three days a week, and she has also started operating her own lending library out of her home for friends and neighbors. She charges a small fee on each book and uses the money to purchase new ones. She is also taking literature classes at the local university with the hopes of earning a masters degree within the next five years. Although the additional income may be somewhat minimal now, she is still able to afford the many books she would like to have and she is doing more reading now than ever before—all of which, she hopes, will make her a top college literature teacher someday.

Another man listed foreign travel at the top of his list. Since he is a teacher with free summers, he now plans to work as a tour guide for a travel agency.

Exercise 2: The Daydream List

I hope you love this assignment as much as I do. Kick off your shoes, lean back in your chair, close your eyes, and allow your mind the delicious treat of daydreaming. Think about anything you would like to see, do, or become. Do you see yourself taking a Caribbean cruise, running for political office, building a dream house, or winning the Pillsbury Bake-off? Perhaps you would like to write a best-selling novel, or star in a motion picture.

Spend at least ten minutes on this reverie and then turn to page 210 of your workbook section to record your ideas.

One man who has been a great influence and example in my life is John Goddard. When he was only fifteen years old he knew what he wanted to do for the rest of his life. He wanted to live out daydreams—127, to be exact. Among other things, he wanted to explore the Nile, ride an ostrich, read the Bible from cover to cover, and write an article for *National Geographic*. He also set goals to do 200 sit-ups and twenty chin-ups daily.

By the age of fifty-two, reported *People* magazine, Mr. Goddard had lived out 105 of his dreams and was earnestly involved in making the others come true. When I read about his success, I resolved to create my own list and to start working on it immediately. To date I have achieved thirty-seven of those dreams, including building a dream home, writing three best-selling books, tripling my income, and having two children after being told I could never bear a child. This book is number thirty-eight on my list. When this is completed, I have many more dreams to work on.

Truly, the act of making a daydream list has had a profound effect on my life. But it also has had an important effect on some of my workshop participants.

One young woman who took my workshop a few years ago was feeling terribly frustrated with her life. She had graduated from college expecting to marry and rear a family. When this didn't happen immediately she tried to survive as a secretary. Unfortunately, she found out her bosses could survive better without her than with her. In fact she had just lost her tenth job in two years when I met her.

When we examined her daydream list, we discovered that there were no fantasies about success as a secretary. Instead she wanted a different kind of excitement. She longed to be writing interesting articles and interviewing fascinating celebrities. That night she went home, got out her writing supplies, and wrote a letter to Joe Namath asking for an interview. She told him that what she lacked in experience she made up for in charm. Namath gave her the interview. She sold her piece and was well on her way to success.

Another woman came into my workshop having signed divorce papers the day before. On her daydream list were plans for a new house, a desire to start her own business, and a wish to become a talented pianist. In the process of achieving her goals, she became re-enthused about life, attracted a wonderful man, and is now happily sharing her dreams and aspirations with him.

Of course, the simple act of making a daydream list will not automatically make your dreams come true, but it is a start. Before you can create, you must have an idea. The more specific your dreams are, the better your chances of turning them into realities.

When I interviewed Dr. Maxwell Maltz, author of the bestseller *Psycho-Cybernetics* (Englewood Cliffs, NJ: Prentice-Hall, 1960) he stated that when we daydream, we are using the right side of our brain, which is our creative side. Research has indicated that the use of the right side of the brain differs somewhat between men and women. Mental functions are organized somewhat differently. Men seem to have more laterality, which means their mental functions are under separate control by the right or left side of the brain. On the other hand, women use more of the right side of their brain or function through both sides of the brain. The right side of your brain is your creative, intuitive side. (Could this be a scientific explanation for the validity of reputed "women's intuition"?) Burt Reynolds stated that his career soared when he learned to use more of the right side of his brain. It helped him become more creative.

Exercise 3: Acknowledging Your Needs

All of us have needs. The items included on your daydream list undoubtedly represent many of them. Perhaps that desire to go on an African safari will meet a need for travel or adventure. The dream of being a successful entertainer may satisfy your craving for a little prestige or popularity. Studies have shown that most world-class athletes have a deep need to be number one in something. They also have a need for lots of competition in their lives.

Fortunately, most needs can be fulfilled with a variety of activities. For example, consider the numerous ways you could add new experience to your life, especially if your occupation is boring yet provides you with a good living. What can you do to really feel better about yourself? I'm too survival-conscious to advise someone to quit his job without a better one lined up, but many people get a great deal of satisfaction outside of their profession, gaining needed balance in their lives. The options are practically unlimited. You could sign up for a course in belly dancing or karate, take up skydiving, learn something about auto mechanics, or even start a new career. You could try some new recipes, redecorate your house, take a course in wilderness survival, or go for a ride in a hot-air balloon.

Recently I met a woman who had spent the majority of her life in a university environment. She had completed work on her masters and was now contemplating a doctorate. But after consulting her needs, she decided there were other areas of her life that had long been neglected. She wanted to become more creative. To do so, she decided to learn the art of flower arranging and to get some training as a beautician.

I have designed a questionnaire (pages 211 and 212 of your workbook section) to make you aware of your most vital needs and desires. Give each statement a numerical rating between 1 and 5. A 5 would indicate that this particular desire is an important part of your current inner make-up. After you finish the exercise, go back and put a star by the most important needs that are not being met to your satisfaction and fulfillment.

Excercise 4: The Perfect Day

Suzi, the busy mother of two young children, wrote, "On my perfect day I wake up without the aid of an alarm clock and I take as long as I want to get ready for the day. My husband and I are in a beautiful, elegant hotel, so we order breakfast from room service. In this fantasy I spend the entire day with my husband, being pampered and spoiled. We go shopping and I buy dozens of beautiful clothes. In the evening, we go to the ballet and then go dining and dancing at some romantic restaurant. In my perfect day I also get a manicure, a pedicure, and a massage. Throughout the entire experience I never feel rushed or hurried."

Designing a perfect day is another wonderful and unique way of revealing our deepest needs. For example, Suzi realized she had a need to spend more time on herself without constant interruptions. She also needed to feel unrushed. She explained, "In the mornings I almost feel like a robot, rushing around to get myself ready, helping the kids get dressed, fixing breakfast, and then car-pooling everyone to school."

Barbara Sher, author of *Wishcraft* (New York: Viking Press, 1979), suggests there are three important elements to consider when we design our own perfect days:

1. **The place.** In what kind of environment or situation do you visualize yourself? A beach home, a mountain retreat, a busy office, a fully equipped workshop, or a "dream home"? Perhaps you would like to spend your perfect day in your own home.

You may even choose to spend your perfect day in a variety of places. One woman decided she would spend her morning working hard on a romantic novel and then in the late afternoon she would jet off to San Francisco for a night out on the town.

Another woman said she would love to spend her perfect day at home if there was just one addition—a large, soundproof room where she could spend a few hours in quiet contemplation without interruption from her children.

2. The itinerary. What are your activities and events for the day? Is it a time of total leisure or hard work? Do you spend it doing the kinds of things you would normally be involved with in your career, or are you engaged in different activities? One young salesman who took the workshop saw himself as an attorney working on an exciting case. A student saw herself as a dress designer working in her own studio with famous clients coming to look at her originals.

3. The people. Whom do you spend your day with? How much time do you spend alone and how much do you spend with others? You will probably want to have some of your favorite family members and friends with you, but there are many other individuals you might want to include.

Keep in mind that you become like the people you surround yourself with. For that reason, it is important that you choose positive, stimulating, loving friends who are motivating, optimistic, and encouraging. One young homemaker said she would like to expose her children and family to the people who are making things happen in the world. On her perfect day she decided to have the President and his family over for a barbecue. Perhaps you don't have specific individuals in mind, but you know the types of people you would like to have around: celebrities, artists, athletes, people from other cultures, and so on.

One of my husband's favorite coaches is Frank Kush, former football coach at Arizona State University. I noted the interest with which he followed ASU's games and the admiration he showed toward this legendary man. He would go on the defensive if anyone made negative comments about a particular off game, and loved watching Kush being interviewed. Once he came home from a trip excited because Kush was on his flight, even though he didn't get to sit next to him.

I realized when trying to decide on a birthday present for my husband—and after being with someone for twenty birthdays you tend to run out of ideas for creative gifts—that an hour with football coach Frank Kush would be a memorable event for him. Luckily, Kush agreed, and during my husband's surprise party he answered the doorbell and there stood Frank Kush. He turned to me grinning ear to ear and said, "He looks just like Frank Kush." I then advised him he had three hours to talk football as my special birthday gift. I think if you asked my husband about his favorite birthday, he would recall that special occasion—because of the people.

On page 213 of your workbook section you will find plenty of space to assemble your perfect day. After this task. is completed, analyze the day and decide which needs are currently missing from your life. You may want to turn these needs into goals and objectives. Also, occasionally think about people you would like to know better. Remember, we attract the things we think about.

Exercise 5: Your Five-Year Goals

I would like you to shake hands mentally with yourself in five years, because what you visualize and where you see yourself is the person you will become. Earlier in the chapter we talked about the importance of knowing where you would like to be in five years. As Daneke pointed out, there is a difference between predicting ("If I go on as I am now, this will happen") and planning ("This is where I would like to be"). In this assignment, don't predict—*plan*.

Unfortunately, statistics show that less then five percent of the people in the world set out to conquer life with a definite plan of action. The majority of individuals simply live their life from day to day with no real direction. Instead of taking the initiative to set goals and objectives, they let someone else do it for them—their parents, their bosses, the government, or the economy. When an individual develops a real plan of action and a direction in his or her life, incredible things can happen. When I worked as a social worker in Florida, my job required that I visit the homes of indigent clients to determine eligibility for assistance. On a particularly hot day, as I was visiting an elderly client, I sat down next to him on the front porch of his daughter's home. He was sitting there dressed in overalls and smoking a corncob pipe, seemingly in a reflective mood. He was a former sharecropper who reportedly had worked hard all of his life but never worked smart; because he had not made plans for retirement, he was now destitute and forced to live with his children. I was always very concerned about my clients, and as we visited I asked him where he had thought he would be at this time of his life when he was a young man. He studied my question, looked around the front porch of his daughter's house, and commented, "Lady, I thought I'd be right where I am." I realized then the *power* of seeing yourself in the future.

Once I asked Dolly Parton, who was raised in poverty in Sieverville, Tennessee, if as a small child she ever imagined she would become rich and famous. She answered that she *always* knew she would someday become who she is today. It made the poverty bearable for her to believe some day she would have so much more.

Come on, be honest with yourself. Aren't you where you are right now because that is what you expected of yourself? We become what we think about all day long!

Recently I read about a man named Marc Kreiner. Five years ago he was a soda jerk for Baskin-Robbins. Today he promotes and produces disco records. He owns a $4.5 million beach home, a Rolls Royce, a Porsche, and two $80,000 Cadillacs.

Another favorite success story is that of Paula Nelson, often called "the corporate whiz kid." In ten years, with only six *days* of college behind her, Paula succeeded in co-founding three manufacturing companies, authoring a best-seller entitled *The Joy of Money* (Stein and Day, 1975), and landing herself a job as a financial consultant on the "Today Show," seen coast to coast by millions of viewers every morning.

Neither of these people was any smarter or brighter than you or me, and they didn't start out with great financial assets. But they did know what they wanted from life and they weren't afraid to pursue it. They had more than a good attitude; they had a burning desire.

On page 214 of your workbook, you will find a five-year blueprint. Describe everything as you would like it to be in five years. Write about your home, its location, and its furnishings. Discuss the work or the projects you have chosen to be involved with. List your salary and your assets. Describe the way you spend your leisure time and the quality of your relationships. Be as specific as possible, for you are planting ideas that will develop to the extent you think about them. Remember, you become what you think about all day long.

Of course, these five-year goals are not written in concrete. You can always change your mind—in fact you probably will. The important thing to realize is that in order to win the very best in life, you must start with a goal. From there you can develop a road map and a plan of action that will lead you to your destination.

Also, be aware of goals you have that you may not have acknowledged in the past. Recently I did a program on goal setting and improving self-esteem for a group of municipal employees. Afterwards a woman approached me looking quite concerned, asking me if I could recommend a good book on goal setting, for she really didn't have any goals. My immediate reaction was that I had failed her in my presentation, but I realized that this was not really true. A person gets from a book, a seminar, a lecture, or whatever they come in contact with, that which they truly need and are looking for.

Before making any recommendations I asked her to tell me about herself. She stated she had been married for fifteen years, was recently divorced, and would never depend on anyone else in her life. (What did she tell me? Goal number one.) I didn't comment, except to say, "Tell me more." She said she had lost fifteen pounds, had ten more pounds to lose and that she would never be overweight again. I still didn't say much except, "Great, then what do you plan to do?" but I realized this also was a goal. She then said she wanted to buy a new wardrobe of beautiful designer clothes. She had never before been able to justify buying expensive clothes as she had always been overweight and felt she would not look good enough to show them off.

I then started smiling for several reasons. One was for my own benefit. I really had done a good job in my seminar. I then pointed out to her that she had just shared three goals in less than five minutes that were just as important to her as a goal anyone would have for their future happiness and success. She just never had looked at what she desired as a goal. Goals are relative to an individual's needs. No one can determine what is important to someone else. We are all a product of our own awareness. That is what makes us so unique. No one is smarter or less intelligent than you or me. It is just that some people are more or less aware.

Exercise 6: Your Special Mission on Earth

It has been said that the happiest people are those who spend time trying to improve or better the world in some unique way. I believe this is true. Thus far, we have spent a great deal of time thinking about the things you personally want and need to be happy in life. But now it is time to think about the contributions you would like to make to others.

At this point you may be wondering just exactly what unique gift you have to offer mankind. I am reminded of a story told by a man who felt he had no talents in life. As he grew up he observed the other members of his family and noticed they were especially talented in music or art. Unfortunately, he had no such gifts. He then looked at his friends who were gifted athletically or intellectually, but he concluded he was "just average" in both of these areas. Finally, he realized he had one special quality that could be shared with others—his enthusiasm. In fact he was capable of adding enthusiasm to any group he became involved with.

In his youth he was excited about sports, so he used his enthusiasm to make the team and help them to win the championship. In his later life he became very service-oriented. He realized he didn't have the talents of some individuals. He couldn't invent a cure for cancer or write great music to be enjoyed by all, but he could always lend his enthusiasm, his dedication, and his ability to work hard for any organization that was doing something to better the world. Each person has the ability to help someone else.

Consider the areas of life you feel most concerned about and then analyze what needs to be done. On page 215 of the workbook, you will find space to list your alternatives and goals. Let me tell you what some individuals have done after asking themselves what contribution they could make.

A homemaker with a large family wanted to be of service in some way but felt rather tied down because of her children. However, she decided there always was room for one more, so she and her husband became involved in the foster child program. They often take infants who cannot live at home into their own home for a few weeks or several months.

One doctor who worked with young cancer patients asked himself what these children could be doing to serve others. His answer was that they could help other cancer victims. He organized a program to allow each young child to contact other patients to give them encouragement and emotional support. He told me that he observed, for the first time, remission in his patients who became involved in helping others. They seemed to have more reason to live. Knowing that others needed them triggered an immune mechanism in their bodies to fight for their own lives. We're only beginning to learn the healing effects of our minds.

A retired school teacher visited a relative in a nursing home and noticed that the quilts and blankets were in poor repair. Being a quilting enthusiast, she went home and made several small lap robes and quilts as a donation to the patients. No one can visit a nursing home without becoming aware of how others need them. You have so much that is desperately needed by so many, many people. Your very presence is valuable to someone who is lonely.

As you can see from these examples, each individual has a unique service to share with others, a place where his or her talents and contributions can be appreciated. Do a mental personal evaluation right now. Realize that most people have the same needs as you. Give to others what you want most, whether it is love, kindness, companionship, or understanding. I promise it will be returned to you tenfold.

I'm convinced we're all here for that reason. Edgar Cayce once said, "The way to Heaven is on the arm of the man you help." Heaven is right here for the person who lives with that philosophy. Start today by becoming more aware of how you can help others. Making people feel better about themselves is the greatest gift you can give them. All it takes is a little effort and sincerity on your part.

Cavette Robert, one of the greatest public speakers in America, once said to me, "Everyone has an invisible sign on them. It says, 'Make me feel important.'" The greatest gift we can give to anyone is to recognize his unique and special qualities and then let him know we see him.

Exercise 7: Establishing Your Top Priorities

Now that you have examined your needs, your desires, your daydreams, and the contributions you would like to make to mankind, I would like you to turn to page 216 of your workbook and consider four questions:

1. What are your three most important lifetime goals?
2. If you only had six months to live, what would be your major objectives?
3. How would you be spending time today if you could select from any of your goals or activities?
4. How would you live your life if you knew you could not fail?

If we have missed any important dreams or goals in the previous exercises, this is a good way to discover them. It is also a good way to set priorities.

It has been said that we all have enough time to do what we really want to do, but in reality, none of us really knows how much time we will have on earth. That is why it is so important to set priorities. Once we have achieved the important things, we can begin to spend our time on less important activities.

BEGINNING YOUR FUTURE

All of the exercises you have completed in this chapter can help you come to grips with where you currently are in life and where you want to go. But now you have to make a decision. Do you want to continue as you have up to this point or do you want to change direction? If you decide to continue on the same path, you will find lots of information in the upcoming chapters to help you do it better. But if you have an imagination full of dreams and fantasies, take my word for it—you can turn those new goals into brilliant realities.

3
Setting Goals and Making Dreams Come True

Plan your work, work your plan.
—Author unknown

I noticed her in one of the first workshops I ever conducted as a time-management consultant. Her name was Amanda. She was a slender, rather shy woman in her early thirties. I liked the enthusiasm she radiated. She had just finished her first assignments in daydreaming and recognition of needs. She now had a question.

"I know what I want from life. In five years I would like to be an executive for the corporation I work with. I want to boost my income so I can afford some of the finer things in life, but most of all I would like to feel like a real asset to the company. I would like to be making decisions and feeling as if I were part of the action. I like the power that goes with being an executive. Right now I am just a secretary. The only thing I am valued for is my shorthand and typing. I have no education and no experience as an executive. How can a person like me ever achieve such an objective?"

I reassured Amanda that such an objective was possible and that other women had achieved similar successes.

"Well, what is the secret?" asked Amanda. "Where do I start?"

"With goals," I replied, "clear, precise, short-term goals. Right now I could give you five simple goals to start with—any of which would get you well on the road to your dream destination."

In this chapter we are going to discuss the importance of short-term goals, the ways you can make them work for you, and I am going to share with you the five goals I gave Amanda to help her get started. Let's begin by considering why goals are so important to your success.

Ty Boyd, a friend and fellow member in the National Speaker's Association, tells a story about an interview with the late H. L. Hunt, one of the wealthiest men in our country. On this occasion Ty asked Mr. Hunt the secret of his success. He said there were four things you had to do:

First, you've got to decide what you want.
Second, you've got to decide what you're willing to give up.
Third, you've got to then set priorities.
Fourth, you've got to be about your work.

What does it mean to "be about your work?" It means to get out of bed in the morning and take action. It means you've got to take whatever physical steps are necessary to make that goal a reality. As Mr. Hunt said, "If you don't do number four, the first three won't get you anyplace."

Most people can do the first three, but when it comes to number four on that list, they come to a sudden halt. If you do not consider yourself a success at this point in your life, be honest with yourself. Have you really worked for what you've dreamed about obtaining? Has the world shortchanged you, or do you realize and admit you are where you are because that is exactly where you want to be or deserve to be? Each of us must face this cold, hard fact. We determine our own destiny.

I'm always amused with friends that consult with psychics

to find out what is in store for them in the future. They should be telling the psychic what to expect of the future, on the basis of the course of action they've chosen.

THE IMPORTANCE OF GOALS

Goals save you time. They help to channel and direct your energy and enthusiasm. They provide an immediate purpose to work toward. They give you a reason to get out of bed in the morning.

Did you ever wake up on a Saturday morning without a plan of action? You had nothing on the agenda and nothing to look forward to. Did you accomplish very much that day? Probably not. You may have wasted valuable hours and retired for the evening with no sense of satisfaction or accomplishment.

Goals enable you to make the most of each day. When you have a goal there is always something to get excited about. Energy and enthusiasm can be channeled and used constructively rather than wasted. You actually physically beam with pride when you are focused on a goal.

Another advantage is that goals (especially short-term or minigoals) allow you to have continual success experiences. Not only do you have the satisfaction of looking forward to your big dream, but you can also enjoy many smaller successes along the way.

Consider the child who studies the piano hoping to play in Carnegie Hall one day. A wise teacher will set up small goals to be achieved along the way—giving stars for completion of difficult pieces and awards for special performances.

You may not have a devoted teacher to set up reachable goals, but you can still give yourself continual success experiences to help you stay motivated and determined to reach your objective.

How to Turn Goals into Success Experiences

Many people set goals, but not everyone achieves them. Why? Generally people put off accomplishing their goals because they seem too complex, too time-consuming, or the people just don't know where to get started. In fact, studies have shown that most people will not start a project unless they truly believe it can be finished. At this point you may not be totally convinced of your ability to earn a million dollars or start your own business, but you can build that belief in yourself and your project by giving yourself success experiences. The way to do this is with a short-term goal. Here are some guidelines and suggestions.

1. **Set a goal you can visualize yourself achieving.** Calvin Lehew, a friend of mine from Tennessee who is a successful real estate entrepreneur and motivational speaker on success principles, taught me many years ago that there are three important steps to achieving success, which he learned from reading Dr. Norman Vincent Peale's *The Power of Positive Thinking* (Englewood Cliffs, NJ: Prentice-Hall, 1952). According to Dr. Peale, successful people *picturize*, *prayerize*, and *actualize*.

Calvin had used this theory along with persistence and determination to become a millionaire before he was thirty-five. He advised me to use visualization techniques he had mastered to obtain whatever success I wanted in life. He told me it was important to cut out colored pictures representing my goals and desires, keep them in an easily accessible file, and refer to them frequently to make the object or goal part of my consciousness.

I reflected on how I had used a similar technique while teaching in an impoverished area in Daytona Beach, Florida. I was attempting to motivate my students to stay in school, to get a good education so that someday they could have nice homes and beautiful things such as china, crystal, and silver. They looked at me with blank expressions. Why should they work hard for such possessions? They had never been exposed to such luxuries. They were drinking out of fruit jars at home. When I talked about how beautiful and desirable crystal was, it confused them. Realizing this, I planned field trips, taking them to fine department stores where they could handle beautiful crystal, china, and silver. Then, for the first time, it was part of their consciousness. They were aware of some of the rewards for hard work and success. Before that they had had no motivation.

You can raise your consciousness in the same way with colored pictures and a healthy imagination.

The story is told of a young teenager who had the dream of becoming a doctor. But the dream was in jeopardy because he was failing his high school science class. He went to his advisor for counseling.

"What do you want to become in life?" asked the counselor.

"A doctor," was the youth's reply.

The counselor described the long hours of study and dedication that would be required to complete medical school successfully.

"Can you see yourself meeting those requirements?" questioned the counselor.

"No," replied the boy.

Then the counselor described the tough premed courses and grades the young man would be required to achieve in college.

"Can you see yourself paying the price to attain that kind of success?"

Again the young man could not.

Finally the young counselor asked whether the boy would be willing to put in a few extra hours every night to improve his high school science grades.

"Yes!" the boy responded excitedly.

As the story goes, the young man put in the extra study hours, passed his science class with flying colors, and graduated at the top of his class. He went to college, was accepted for medical school, and is now a practicing physician.

The boy was able to actualize his daydream because he started with an achievable goal. He had to visualize his success before he could follow through with proper action. If you can't visualize yourself achieving the objective, then select another short-term goal.

2. Set a goal that is measurable and concrete. When setting a goal, ask yourself these questions:

Is my goal specific?
Will I be able to see the difference after I have achieved it?
Is it measurable?

Generally speaking, accomplishing a goal requires a specific action; you are probably thinking in generalities that will be difficult to translate into a success experience.

During a recent workshop, one participant was determined to achieve the goal of being a better father to his children.

"That's a good objective," I explained, "but it's a rather vague-sounding goal. Why not think of a specific, measurable action you could start with this week."

After discussing several alternatives, the father finally decided he would try to smile and give a genuine compliment to each of his three children every day for a week. Every day he would tell each child that he loved him, even if it was in a casual manner, as they departed for school or when he returned home from work.

Seven days later he reported back, saying his experiment had been a success. His new goal was to spend one half hour with each child sometime during the week participating in an activity that the child would especially enjoy.

Specific goals bring about specific results. These results give you a positive successful experience and they let you know you are right on target for achieving your objective.

3. Set goals that will open the door to opportunity. Always try to choose goals that are open-ended, leading you successfully upward. Consider the approach of Benjamin Franklin. Although Franklin's formal schooling ended when he was ten, he spent his nights studying arithmetic. At the age of twelve he added formal writing exercises. Later, in his teens, he studied foreign languages, including French, Italian, Spanish, and Latin. With such a firm foundation in education, Franklin was able to move from poverty to great wealth. And because of his earlier goals, he was able to achieve success as a scientist, inventor, statesman, and writer.

When Paula Nelson, the corporate whiz kid mentioned in Chapter 2, decided to move from "secretary" to "successful businesswoman," she also started with her education. Although she did not return to college, she began following what she loosely termed "the Paula Nelson financial education program."

Says Ms. Nelson, "I wanted to gain the best information available, so I attended seminars offered by stockbrokers, read numerous books and magazines on the subject, and continually asked questions. I spent time observing successful businessmen in their day-to-day activities, listening to the way they handled themselves in their conversations and meetings." It was from these early learning goals that Paula was able to move successfully into the business world and achieve her great success.

4. **Select a general time frame for the completion of each goal.** Your tasks will seem less overwhelming if you set yourself deadlines, and they will help you avoid procrastination. For example, when I decided to write this book, I set minideadlines: a deadline for my chapter outline; a weekly finishing date for each chapter; and additional deadlines for the rewrites. Deadlines make procrastination impossible. If necessary, commit yourself to another individual. Tell this person what you will achieve and when you will complete it. When it is broken down into segments, you have faith it is obtainable.

5. **Give yourself rewards as you complete each goal.** Always have something to look forward to. I reward myself by spending more time with my children. They bring more

satisfaction and joy to my life than anything else I could imagine. Spending more time with them is an incentive for me to accomplish my tasks quickly.

Some individuals like to reward themselves with a short vacation at the end of a difficult task. Others are satisfied simply to record their results and observe their progress. One woman I know keeps a journal of her daily successes. She claims it has the same effect as giving a child a star for learning a new piano piece.

I once asked a seventy-six-year-old guest author on my daily television show what motivated her to do a book tour, since I knew how grueling promotional tours can be. She commented that when the tour was over she got to enjoy her piece of the pie, which was a Caribbean cruise. The pie represented her whole life, which is sometimes divided up among all the people who demand your time and energy. She had learned to save some of the pie for herself.

6. Set goals that will not allow for procrastination. The excuses for not completing goals that I hear from workshop participants are many and varied.

"I am too busy to study now."

"I just can't seem to find the time."

"I can't make time for this project until after the holidays."

Instead of making excuses, set different goals. If you haven't got an hour to spend, try finding half an hour, or even ten minutes a day, to apply toward your goals. The pace will be slower, but even crawling is better than standing still.

We procrastinate about unpleasant things, griping and complaining all day long, somehow hoping they will resolve themselves or someone else will do them. I say, "Learn to eat the crust first." Let me explain.

Once I had a friend over for dinner and I served pie for dessert. Now, many years ago I learned how to serve a piece of pie properly. You use your left hand and place the pie in front of your guest with the wedge's point toward him.

I noticed my friend turn the pie around and start eating from the back. When I asked him to explain why he turned the pie around to start eating, he said, "Rita, I love pie, but I've never liked the crust. I want to get the crust over with so I can enjoy the pie."

Whatever it is that you procrastinate about because the task is undesirable—do that task first. Otherwise, you'll make yourself miserable by the delay. See how much better you'll feel if you just go ahead and get it over with. The good fairy only appears in nursery rhymes. No one will, or even can, do certain things for you. If this delay makes you feel worse—get it over with. Eat the crust first.

When I made the decision to become a top time-management consultant, I resolved that I would take time to do something every day toward the accomplishment of my goal. Perhaps it would be to read a book, write an article, set up a workshop, or meet with other people in my field—but every day I had to do something.

I have accomplished my objectives by grabbing five minutes here, ten minutes there, and even brainstorming for ideas while driving the car, making notes while waiting for the lights to change. When I am with friends I often turn our conversation to time management, asking them for their own success stories and tips for better management of time.

I promise you, goals can be accomplished even with an already crowded schedule. Just be aware of your left-over minutes and be prepared to use them wisely (more about that subject in Chapter 4).

7. **Attack all your goals with enthusiasm.** Consider the tasks at hand and ask yourself the question, "How would I be completing this goal if I had enthusiasm?" And then ask yourself, "Would I accomplish it more quickly? More easily? With less frustration?" Imagine the results in your mind, and then match your performance with the vision.

Believe it or not, by adding enthusiasm to a task, you can save time. I asked three women to choose five tasks that needed to be completed before they could move ahead on their five-year goals and objectives. They all chose tasks that they had already been procrastinating on. I explained that even though they felt no enthusiasm for the activities, they had to pretend they were enthusiastic. The result was that at the end of the week, each woman had completed her set of tasks and could now move on to something more pleasant. Enthusiasm, even pretended enthusiasm, does make a difference.

8. **Learn to make your daydream goals top priority.** Every morning ask the question, "What is the most important thing I can accomplish in relation to this goal?"

Make it the first task of the day. Don't let the lower priority activities break your concentration or momentum. Try getting up one hour earlier, especially if you have small children and are hard-pressed for time. You can accomplish a lot before the family becomes demanding and noisy in the morning. Or eliminate a nonproductive activity, such as watching television, reading the newspaper, going to a movie.

You may even spend all of your free time working on one task, but you will still have the satisfaction of knowing that it was the most important.

9. **Find ways to enjoy working on each short-term goal.** Ask a winner whether he enjoyed the road to his daydream destination, and he will probably answer yes!

Bruce Jenner, the fine American athlete who won the gold medal for the decathlon in the Olympics of 1976, trained for eight years to achieve his goal. During the last four years the gold medal became his obsession. His routine was one of discipline, sacrifice, and deliberate action. He learned to calculate everything. He set his own short-term goals, achieved them, and then moved on to greater ones. In commenting on the long process, Jenner wrote, "I loved the training." Do you love achieving your goals?

You can begin to enjoy the life of a goal seeker by allowing yourself to become completely absorbed in your work. Learn to control your mind. Don't let it wander to other thoughts when you are working on your dream. Try to stay on focus. Develop and practice internal discipline. Rejoice over your progress and accomplishments.

10. **Evaluate your performance.** I ask workshop participants to rate their performance on a daily basis. Using a scale of 1 to 10, or ratings such as *excellent, good, fair, poor,* clients learn to be continually responsible for turning in a good performance.

You must learn to evaluate your performance at the end of an hour, the end of a day, and the end of a week. Evaluation will help improve your personal performance, work, creative talents, and even your communication skills. Constant evaluation is one key to making your short-term goals work for you.

THE SUCCESS PYRAMID

Visualize a pyramid. At the top of this magnificent structure is your daydream or five-year goal. Let each block of the edifice represent a short-term or minigoal you have achieved. It may be developing a new skill, overcoming a bad habit, or magnifying your talents through a fine opportunity.

Now imagine the first short-term goal you would like to work on. On pages 217 and 218 of the workbook section you will find your own short-term goal sheet and a sample sheet that has already been completed. Fill in the blanks and use it as a guideline to help you achieve your first minigoal.

Five Minigoals to Get You Started

If you are still uncertain as to which step to take first, here are five possible alternatives, any of which should help you become actively involved in working toward your goal.

1. Seek the best information available in relation to your daydream or objective. In the long run it will save you time and also act as a road map toward the completion of your task. Try to evaluate what will be required in terms of personal, financial, and other resources. This advance knowledge will help you prepare to handle opportunities as they come.

Recently a group of college students were given an assignment to help them prepare effectively for their futures. They were required to write to four hundred companies that usually hired graduates from their business college and inquire what qualities they as potential employees would have to exhibit on their résumés and interviews. The students asked the companies to rate twenty-five different items such as personality characteristics, grades, family background, habits, special skills, communication talents, and leadership qualities.

When their assignment was completed the students knew how to prepare for their future jobs. They felt confident about their interviews and realized they had a distinct advantage as they competed with other students for top positions.

2. Choose some good role models. Start by compiling a list of individuals who have made similar dreams or goals come true. Each personality will have a different story to tell. Each will manifest a different set of strengths and attributes, but from your study you should be able to gain lots of motivation and a few tricks of the trade to help you achieve success.

If possible, set up a personal interview with your role models. Plan your questions in advance. Be prepared with a tape recorder or notebook. There are many subjects you might ask them to discuss, but consider using some of the following questions to help you get started:

· What is the most effective way you found to use your time? How much time did you devote to your goal on a daily or weekly basis?

- What were your greatest strengths or talents for accomplishing your goal?
- What weakness did you have to overcome? What new habits did you have to develop?
- What kind of education do you recommend to someone who wants to achieve the kind of success you have enjoyed?
- What was the ratio of talent to hard work?
- What kind of sacrifices did you have to make along the way?
- What problems did you have to face before your objectives could be accomplished?
- What kind of philosophy of life do you have?
- Looking back on the way you achieved your success, is there anything you would have done differently?
- Did you enjoy the pursuit of your goal?
- What was a typical schedule for you in the trek toward your goal?
- What experiences and learning in your background best prepared you for success?
- Did you ever define your goals in specifics?
- Now that you have achieved your desires, what do you enjoy most about being on top?
- Was expectation ever greater than realization?

Study your role models for their strengths. Analyze their personalities for particular attributes such as dedication, hard work, or perseverance. But don't assume that they are totally perfect. Use your role models as guides, but don't put them on pedestals.

3. Consult with the experts in the field you are pursuing. You might want to talk with coaches, teachers, counselors, or other individuals offering special services that can contribute to the formation of your total goal or objective.

Before you decide to put yourself into the hands of anyone for help, however, do a complete study of all resource people available to you. Experts usually charge money for their services. You must be especially careful to select people who are honest and knowledgeable and who, above all, will give their best to help you achieve your goal.

Whether you are seeking the services of a music teacher, coach, agent, or plastic surgeon, don't be afraid to study their backgrounds before making a choice. When interviewing an expert:

- Compare the costs of their services with others who offer similar expertise.
- Check their background. Where did they get their training? Whom have they helped? How long have they been in business?
- How much of a business do they have now? How much time can they devote to your particular needs? How much do they seem to care about you?
- Are there contracts to sign? Have a lawyer check them over first. Know exactly what will be expected from both parties.
- Keep your total objectives clear and focused. Know exactly what this expert can offer you in relation to your total goal.
- Don't be afraid to check them out with the Better Business Bureau. Even better, ask to interview others who have utilized their services. Don't make any decisions or sign any contracts before you have studied all of the alternatives.

Remember, too, that experts will often disagree, especially where costs (time, money, and sacrifice) are involved. Expect this in advance. Only by questioning all the experts will you be able to gain the best information and choose the one who can most successfully help you achieve your goals.

Six years ago, a young man named Ken decided to make his dream come true. He wanted to be one of the best trumpet players in the country. He wanted to be qualified to give clinics, concerts, and teach the instrument on a college level. But at the time of his decision he was twenty years old and had only one year of trumpet lessons behind him.

Before he spent any more time or money on his goal he wisely decided to consult with the experts in the field. He began talking with several performers and consulted with top trumpet players. Ultimately he was referred to one of the best trumpet teachers in the country, Claude Gordon. Mr. Gordon explained the road would be long and arduous. It would mean practicing three hours a day, seven days a week. It would require bimonthly trips from Phoenix to Los Angeles for trumpet lessons and there would be another financial outlay for the best instrument and good music. In addition, Ken would have to get his masters degree to qualify as a teacher on a college level. He would also have to search continually for opportunities to perform and play with groups. Although Mr. Gordon warned Ken that it would mean at least ten years of constant dedication and determined effort, he decided to pursue his dream. He's been following the road set out by his teacher for the past six years. Every morning he gets up at five and practices for three hours. He tra.els from Phoenix to Los Angeles twice a month for his lessons. He now has a masters degree and is considering getting a doctorate. There is every indication that Ken will be able to achieve his goal, but if he hadn't found the best teacher to begin with he might never have paid the price or set the right goals to make his dream come true.

4. Do your homework. Whenever I don't know something I go to the library for the answers. This is an especially good way to get started on your goal if you are too shy to interview role models or experts. At the library you can find books, magazines, and periodicals—all of which might have information pertaining to your needs. To find out what is available:

- Check your local public library. If there is a college or university nearby, check out their libraries too. Don't be afraid to talk to the librarian or one of the assistants if you need help or advice in using the library's resources.
- When you read the literature, check the date it was written. If a publication is over five years old, try to find something more up to date.
- Check each book's bibliography and references. This will often lead you to other printed information.
- Ask your local librarian whether any pamphlets on your subject are put out by the federal or state government.
- Study the literature in the same way you would study the experts. Ask questions like, "What are the author's credentials for writing this book? What are his sources of information? Does this writer disagree with others who have written on the same subject?"

Information in print can be a great help to you and usually costs little. Most books are well researched, but don't assume everything you read is true. Only by seeking out all information and checking all sources can you get a realistic picture of the road ahead.

5. Study those who have lost the battle.   This may sound like a strange way to begin working toward a goal, but it can ultimately be very helpful as you plot your own route. If your five-year goal is to get accepted into medical school, you already know what kinds of grades will be expected. But competition is still very high, and many fail to get into medical school. Why? Talking with those who have failed to get into medical school or to achieve a similar goal can help you determine what pitfalls to avoid so you can learn from their mistakes.

If you have an opportunity to talk with such an individual, here are some questions you might ask:

- What kind of plan for success did you design before starting the trek toward your goal?
- Did you have a success team behind you? That is, were you able to gain the support you needed from other individuals to help you in the pursuit of your goal?
- What resources did you lack?
- How did you spend your time?
- Could you have spent your time more productively?
- Did you enjoy the road toward the achievement of your goal or was it drudgery?
- Did you encounter any positive or negative surprises as you pursued your goal?
- If you had to do it all over again, would you still try to achieve your goal, or would you consider it a complete impossibility and direct your interest elsewhere?
- Since I am pursuing a similiar goal, what advice do you have to give me?

Although some individuals will be unwilling to talk about their defeats, many will critique their misfortunes in an effort to help you go all the way in achieving your dreams.

How to Assemble Your Information

As you complete these steps in your pursuit of a goal, you will begin to acquire much information. For help in planning and goal setting, use the fact sheet on page 219 in your workbook.

MOVING AHEAD

Once you have set yourself a challenging and stimulating goal, you will be well on the way to realizing your daydreams and objectives. More important, you will be using your time in a way that can ultimately give you the most happiness and satisfaction. Learn to work consistently. Give yourself a success every day by completing your highest-priority tasks. When we start using time in ways that brings us inner satisfaction and contentment, we also achieve happiness as a by-product.

4

Simplified Time Management
for Complicated People

> Whatever hour God has blessed you with, take it
> with grateful hand, nor postpone your jobs from
> year to year, so that, in whatever place you have
> been, you may say that you lived happily.
>
> —Horace

Some experts say that many of us waste two or more hours every day, and that most people waste time the same way every day! Have you ever stopped to calculate how much of this precious resource you waste in a day, a week, or a month?

The problem is that most of us are not aware of how much time we waste. I used to think that I was using my time effectively just because I was always busy. My schedule was booked from six A.M. until midnight, and I seemed to be always on the go. When I decided to broaden my career and achieve new goals and daydreams, I realized I was going to have to make some changes in the way I spent my time.

I began by studying the experts—people who seem to be highly productive and successful. I found that without exception they had all learned to apply three important principles to their days: *planning, eliminating the nonessential,* and *delegation.*

Let's take a look at each of these principles and then determine how you might apply them to your own situation.

THE VALUE OF PLANNING

No matter how busy you are, you should always take time to plan. Good planning may take only five or ten minutes out of your day, but it can save you hours of frustration and grief. Most important, it can *save you time.*
How should you plan? And what should you plan for? Consider these ideas:
Plan on paper. I do not know of a single successful businessman or businesswoman who does not keep some kind of appointment book, agenda, calendar, or "To do" list with them at all times. Having tried several, I was finally introduced to the Day Timer (put out by Day Timers, Allentown, Pennsylvania 18001). It combines an agenda, a "To Do" list, and a daily diary with a dozen other handy aids, and it comes in a compact notebook that can easily fit into a purse, jacket, or briefcase. I could not function without mine. I highly recommend that you purchase one, or at least note on paper the things you are trying to accomplish. An old Chinese proverb goes: "The palest ink is more powerful than the best memory." Once your errands, appointments, projects, and other ideas are down in black and white, you can free your mind from trying to remember so many details and concentrate on the task at hand.
Plan to make good use of your entire day. Unfortunately, many of us do not use our entire day to the best advantage. Instead, we waste the time when we are most alert on low-priority tasks and try to accomplish important work when we are tired and frazzled.
To determine how you use your total time most effectively, keep track of your physical, mental, and emotional highs and lows for at least a week. Most of us follow cycles or patterns. I function best in the morning, but a friend of mine doesn't really wake up or get her act together until the afternoon. Another workshop participant kept track of her time and found

that from five to six P.M. she was prone to hit a real emotional low. Wanting to make the best use of her time, she decided to use that hour for personal amusement and recreation. She consulted her list of "Favorite Ways to Spend Your Time" and then selected appropriate activities for the hour.

From my own experience and the observation of others I find there is a "good time" to do almost every important task. But everyone's cycle is different. Don't feel you have to jog at six every morning just because your friends do. You may be better off using that hour for sleeping and then planning to stay up an extra few hours in the evening to accomplish your work.

Psychologist Dr. Joyce Brothers once told me that by taking your temperature every three hours you can figure out your peak performance time: it is when you notice a slight increase. If you need help in figuring out your peak time, you may want to take Dr. Brothers's advice.

On page 221 of your workbook you'll find a place to list the tasks and errands you might accomplish whenever you have five or ten minutes to kill. I use my small breaks and waiting time to accomplish errands or to work on details related to my overall goals. I once made a list of all the things I could accomplish in five minutes. I found I could answer a letter, send a postcard to a friend, jog in place for five minutes (of course, I would only do this one in the privacy of my own home), straighten a room, water my plants, load or unload the dishwasher, plan a menu, confirm an appointment, or sew on a button. I have found that most effective people have learned to use their transition or waiting times profitably, and they usually keep a list of activities or details to work on when such moments occur.

Ralph Geddes, a composer and performer who currently travels with the Gatlin Brothers Band, uses intermission time to practice magic tricks and have juggling contests with the other musicians in the group. He uses larger blocks of waiting time to work on a correspondence course.

A writer friend of mine decided to take all of the details and low-priority tasks that generally cluttered up her day, write them on slips of paper, and put them in a cannister. When she wanted to take a five- or ten-minute break from her work, she would draw out a task, complete it, and then return to her writing.

Plan to use your lunch hour most effectively.   Eating out can be a real waste of time. Try brown-bagging it instead. A light lunch will give you more energy for the rest of the afternoon, and, more important, you can use your lunch hour for productive pursuits.

Try making a list of all the things you have always wanted to do with a lunch hour but thought you didn't have time for. Have you wanted to visit a museum, go jogging in the park, sit under a tree and meditate, or get in some quick shopping? What could you do during a lunch hour to contribute to one of your major daydreams or goals?

One young secretary decided to use her lunch hour to take voice lessons, since her goal was to become a professional vocalist some day. Another man decided to bone up on his studies so that he could pass the entrance exam for medical school.

Lunch hour can also be a good time to spend extra time with your children. Consider meeting them at their school for lunch, or having the baby-sitter bring the children to the office for a tour of the building and a picnic in the park.

Plan to use your travel time productively.   I have to spend a lot of time traveling in my car, so I've got it well stocked. I keep a tape deck in it so I can listen to motivational tapes or other things of interest. I've also stocked my glove compartment with postcards, stamps, pens, pencils, note pads, and other useful items (see Chapter 6 for a more complete list). When I get stuck in traffic, I can catch up on personal correspondence, plan menus, make notes for upcoming time-management workshops, and so forth. Many businessmen also have phones installed in their cars. If you generally do a lot of business by phone yet have to spend a lot of time in your car, you might consider it a worthwhile outlay of money.

Plan effectively by setting deadlines. I find both short- and long-term deadlines to be highly motivational in getting my work done. In 1922 a study was made which indicated that the average homemaker devoted about fifty-two hours a week to household tasks. In the 1970s a follow-up study was done by Chase Manhattan Bank which showed that the average full-time homemaker devoted fifty-five hours a week to her housework—a gain of three hours!

The gain occurred not because the modern housewife has more work to do but because she has more time to do it in. This is an example of one of Parkinson's Laws: work expands to fill the amount of time available for it. Although a housewife may spend fifty-five hours a week cleaning, a career woman may spend only twenty-eight hours. The career woman may have as much to do but does not have as many hours available.

The best way to overcome this problem is with a timer. If I have to make a bed, clean a closet, empty the garage, or balance my checkbook, I sometimes set a timer as a challenge to see whether I can do it faster. I have given this tip to several workshop participants, who have reported very positive results.

For larger projects, long-term deadlines can be just as effective. I often challenge myself to see how many important tasks I can complete within a month. Others set effective deadlines by giving themselves rewards such as, "When I finish this thesis, I will treat myself to a nice vacation," or "When I finish the spring cleaning, I will throw a big party for all my friends."

Plan to combine activities. Many activities can easily be combined. I know of one man who listens to tapes of Shakespeare while he shaves in the morning. Another individual memorizes new vocabulary words while jogging.

A young mother told me she combined her household chores with mothering by strapping her four-month-old baby to her back while she did housework. She found she could chat and coo to her baby and let him feel close to her while she did the laundry, dried the dishes, and swept the floor.

Consider all the activities you do now that might possibly be combined. Or examine your goals and objectives to determine how one activity might meet several needs. If you are a gourmet cook who loves to spend time puttering in the kitchen, but you also wish you could spend more time with your children, bring the children in and teach them how to make one of your specialties. The same principle can also work well for married couples. I know of a husband and wife who decided to refinish some antiques together. He had been hoping to spend more time together as a couple and the wife was anxious to do some redecorating. By choosing a mutually compatible activity, they were able to accomplish both goals.

Plan to keep one step ahead of the game. Keeping one step ahead of the game means to anticipate and be prepared. This can be accomplished in several ways.

A university student I know gets a list of all required reading for the fall semester classes and begins studying in the summer. A woman friend of mine starts cooking a week in advance for her dinner parties, making one dish each night and freezing as she goes. She even sets the table the night before. Then it's very easy for her to be a relaxed, gracious hostess, even after working a full day at the office.

Utah's Young Mother of 1978, Michelle Merservy, has made "Keep one step ahead" her motto. She has four preschoolers, and she indicated that it would be impossible to keep up with them if she didn't stay at least one step ahead. In order to achieve this goal, she gives herself a block of time every day when she is free of interruption. Says Mrs. Merservy, "In the afternoon I sew, prepare lessons, plan monthly menus, organize a cupboard, do business work, and so forth, while the children play with their toys."

I stay one step ahead by setting my watch three minutes early, anticipating important deadlines in advance, and by preparing for them early. Remember, in everything we do, preparation precedes power!

Eliminate the nonessential. To determine what is

essential and what is not, consider two important questions on a daily basis:

1. What are my most important goals or objectives? (Consider lifetime goals, five-year goals, and weekly goals.)
2. What effect will each activity on my current "To Do" list have in relation to my goals? Once a value has been placed on each task, prioritize the list and complete the most important items first. Activities that seem to have little or no value should be eliminated if time is short.

Interestingly enough, eighty percent of our success in life generally comes from only twenty percent of our activities. Thus, on an average "To Do" list of ten items, only two tasks will have any substantive value in relation to our real goals or objectives. Yet many of us continue to spend time on low-priority activities. Let's examine some of them.

Television

Unless you plan to become America's number one television critic, you are probably wasting a lot of time in front of the tube. In fact, I would venture to say excessive television viewing has robbed us of more productive time than any other activity or group of activities combined. If watched too much, television can become habit-forming, addictive, and can even cause some harm. Statistics show that the average child watches fifty hours of television a week. Many adults watch more. A recent survey indicated that watching television is America's favorite activity.

Even though I am a television personality and I have great appreciation for the industry, I still contend that there are only three good reasons to watch television. I watch only if it is inspirational, educational, or highly entertaining. If it doesn't fit into one of these categories, I always remind myself that there are a lot of actors and entertainers out there making a perfectly good living at my expense. Why not channel that time into building your *own* success?

Telephone Calls

Next to television, we probably waste more time talking and visiting on the telephone, both in business and at home. Have you ever stopped to calculate how much time you spend on the phone in a single day? We all have different telephone problems.

One woman may have a friend who likes to spend hours chatting on the phone and thus prevents her from accomplishing other important tasks. A businessman may have to deal with clients who continually call to chat about golf scores rather than essential business items. I found that my major problem was unscheduled phone calls. When I was right in the middle of a big project or an important task, someone would call and break my thought process and momentum. I finally solved this problem by becoming my own answering service. When the phone would ring I would pick up the receiver and, imitating a recorded message, say, very slowly and distinctly, "Hello, this is Rita Davenport. I am busy right now, but if you would like to leave a message, I will be happy to get back to you as soon as I can." I found that my callers would go ahead and leave a message, not realizing it wasn't a recorded message. I'd get all the facts and determine if the call was important. If I found it was, I'd say "Hi, I just picked up the phone. I'm so glad you called." (Of course, you can also install a telephone answering machine for less than a hundred dollars which saves you the time of even picking up the phone.) This allows you to use the phone at your own convenience. After all, isn't that why you had it installed? You don't have to be a slave to a telephone unless you allow yourself to be.

Overly long phone calls can also be a problem, but the way you answer the phone can affect the length of the call. I often say to my caller, "Hi, I've just got a few minutes, but it is great to hear from you. What can I do to help you?" I find this breaks through the nonessential chit-chat and brings my caller right to the point. Don't wait for thirty minutes to be honest about your tight schedule. Let them know right away how pressed you are for time. When I am the one initiating the call, I usually make a list of topics I want to cover. This can save time and money, especially when I am calling long distance.

Also, don't elaborate or ask questions if you're on a tight schedule. You'll find an egg timer placed near your phone, boldly displaying the word *Time,* will act as a friendly reminder if you are guilty of spending excessive time on the phone.

When making long-distance calls, I've found it beneficial to cut out and tape to my phone the schedule of phone rates (which you might find in a magazine or perhaps inserted with your phone bill). This offers a handy guide enabling me to see at a glance the most economical time of day to make a long-distance call and the length of time to spend on that call.

Meetings

When you hold a meeting, make sure you start on time, stop on time, and have only key people in attendance. I also recommend that you have an agenda with the items prioritized for discussion. Another tip is to hold short, informal meetings standing up. When I was a schoolteacher I suggested we test this theory by holding our next faculty meeting standing up and then measuring the results. The meeting lasted only twelve minutes, thirty-three minutes shorter than the previous meeting. And we still had covered all the essentials. Why? Just think about it. People come into the room chatting, catching up on the day's activities; they help themselves to a cup of coffee, a few people light up cigarettes, people gradually sit down—still chatting—and a good fifteen minutes have been wasted. I would much rather get business over with, drive home, and then unwind.

I believe an individual should be excused when his or her contribution to the meeting has ended. You can also go to the other person's office for a meeting so you decide when to terminate the encounter by leaving.

Correspondence

The quickest, easiest way to answer a piece of mail is to simply jot down a short reply on the same piece of stationery the request was typed on. It may sound a bit tacky, but you would be surprised at how many professional people use this technique. Also, practice handling a piece of paper just once. This is a tip given to me by Mary Kay Ash, the director of Mary Kay Cosmetics. When she opens a piece of mail, she decides then and there how to handle it. Don't put off till tomorrow what you can do today.

Using a dictating machine is less time-consuming than dictating a letter to your secretary. You might also want to invest in a pocket cassette recorder so you can dictate while traveling.

Excessive Shopping Trips

There are several ways to cut down on shopping time:

1. Always make a weekly menu and try to grocery-shop only once a week. You may also want to purchase household and food items by the case, thus trimming the minutes you have to spend in the store.

2. At the beginning of the year, make a list of all the birthdays and special occasions you will want to remember. Buy your greeting cards in quantity, address the envelopes, and make a notation (in the area where you will put the stamp) of the date each card should be mailed. Now file the cards away in chronological order and store in an accessible location you will see every day. Store stamps nearby too. Each morning just glance at the stack or container of greeting cards and determine which ones should be mailed.

Another way to cut down on excessive shopping trips is to utilize mail-order shopping. Think of the hours and gasoline you'll save, not to mention the headache of crowded stores, especially during the holidays.

I also have a secret shelf where I store gift-wrapped items with a tag on the outside describing the contents. When I need a gift for a special occasion or just to say "thank you," I can quickly go to my shelf instead of making an extra trip to go shopping. This is also a way to pass things on that have been given you but that you cannot use.

3. Try to take care of all of your small errands while traveling to and from work. This will allow you to plan larger blocks of uninterrupted time. Once I get home and into more casual clothes, I like to really relax without having to get dressed again to go out shopping or run an errand.

Visitors

Although it is great to have visitors from time to time, they can really break up your work-flow patterns—both at home and at the office. If you feel especially rushed or have a lot of things you are trying to accomplish, try these tactics:

1. Establish, at the beginning, the amount of time you can spend with your unexpected visitor. I often say, "Hi, it's great to see you. I wish I had more time to visit but I only have a few minutes. I'm just getting ready to go out [for example]. . . . What can I do for you?" You can be courteous and friendly yet firm, letting the visitor know you're happy to see him but you have other demands on your time. Unannounced, unscheduled visitors really don't deserve more. Not letting you know they will be stopping by or calling ahead to schedule an appointment shows a lack of respect for you. Would you drop by to see the governor of your state without first calling ahead for an appointment? No one would expect that, so why shouldn't my time be valued as highly? I used to have this

problem because I had never placed enough value on my time. Now I do. I'm available, but by appointment only. You'll find that people treat you the way you allow them to. Your true friends will not be guilty of such disrespect. They know how busy you are and wouldn't dare interrupt you without calling ahead. They are supportive of your efforts to be effective and successful.

2. Get to the point quickly. Always put an emphasis on serving and helping people meet their needs. Sometimes people just need someone to talk with or want to air their feelings. It is also important to recognize this need in children.

A friend of mine told me about a little neighborhood girl who often felt lonely. Having nowhere else to go, she would come and visit my friend. Unfortunately, this woman was usually busy and had little time to share with the child. But the youngster was persistent. Finally my friend decided that even though she could not entertain the child, she could stop, give the little girl a hug, and spend a minute or two complimenting her. The child, knowing someone cared, would then leave, and my friend was able to return to her work without feeling guilty over the dismissal.

Even if you've only got a few minutes to demonstrate concern for an individual—a child or an adult—smile, shake their hand, give them a pat on the back, and let them know you care. You'll both benefit from the encounter—even though it may be brief.

3. Be firm but pleasant when you terminate a conversation. I often have my assistant interrupt me if someone is keeping me too long. If you don't have an assistant, try standing up and closing with, "Well, it's been great visiting with you. Let me walk you to your car." This shows courtesy and appreciation for the individual's visit and they will hardly know they have been dismissed.

If you are at home, get involved with a task, whether it's cooking, doing some housework, or weeding the garden. Ask your visitor if she would like to help you, because if you must get it done, it will go twice as fast. But if she is there just because she is bored, this will be a signal for her to leave. If she offers to help—which will rarely happen—utilize it with appreciation. If you always stop what you are doing at the whim of uninvited guests, they will be encouraged to drop by uninvited more often.

Obligations

I suggest you eliminate all extracurricular obligations and causes except the ones that mean the most to you. Don't try to spread yourself too thin. Instead, analyze your overall goals and objectives, particularly in the area of service to others. What ways would you really like to help mankind? What causes do you believe in? What kind of work do you enjoy doing? Make these high priorities and learn how to say no to others.

When my first child was born I realized I would have to redefine my priorities. Previously I had been active in many organizations related to my profession. I wrote to each organization explaining that with my new obligations as a parent I would not be able to be as active a member as I had in the past. I did want to continue my career and realized I would have to prioritize my time effectively to be successful as a parent and a professional. I've never regretted that decision and it has given me the confidence to continue saying no to other requests that decrease my focus and concentration. The higher your self-esteem, the easier it becomes to say no to a request that breaks your concentration and focus of power.

Relationships

Reevaluate your friendships. Do you maintain relationships that bring little satisfaction yet take up large amounts of time? Do you try to keep in touch with everyone rather than devoting larger amounts of time to your most treasured friends? If you find your time is being taken up by a lot of relationships that have little meaning to you or your family, consider a gradual cooling off and a building up of the friendships that bring the most pleasure.

The people you surround yourself with have a great effect on your attitude, behavior, performance, and success. Stimulating friends have the ability to raise your expectations as well as your consciousness. We all have the opportunity to learn from the people we come in contact with. I usually use the example in my seminars that you can't soar like an eagle if you're surrounded with turkeys. Another example is: If you want to be skinny, go out to eat with skinny people. You'll notice they eat differently! If you need more physical activity, become friends with a jogger. Sometimes the influence is not obvious, but believe me, it has an effect. That's the reason your parents always wanted you to choose your friends wisely. It's the old saying, "You lie down with dogs, you're bound to get fleas."

Perfectionism

For the most part, perfectionism stifles energy and creativity and wastes time. If you must be a perfectionist, apply it only to your specialty or your most important work in life, but don't let it hinder you the rest of the time.

I once interviewed a famous poetess who had spent years creating beautiful verse while she reared her family. She took great pride in her art and valued her time with her children, but she readily admitted her housework had suffered. She explained, "I tried to analyze what was more important—rearing happy children and writing poetry, or scrubbing kitchen floors. I decided that since my time was limited, I would opt for my creativity and close relationships with my children."

If you have decided to become number one in something, or the world's best anything, by all means make your actions and performance as perfect as you possibly can. But don't let perfectionism become an obsession in other areas of your life.

You will make yourself and everyone else miserable, and you will never have enough time to have fun.

Keep in mind that you are not bionic. It is more important to become an effectiveness expert than an efficiency expert. An efficiency expert will do each job perfectly, spending tedious hours working on each obligation, making sure it is exactly correct.

An effectiveness expert will look at all the jobs that need to be completed and decide which one brings the greatest return on his time and energy. He will do that one first and then go on to the next most worthwhile job.

It is important to do the best you can, giving each obligation your best. After all, when will you have time to do it over? It is better to be an effectiveness expert than an efficiency expert. Remember, an efficiency expert finds the best way to do a job. Effectiveness experts find the best job to do.

The Art of Delegation

Recently I read an article about a free-lance writer who had made $100,000 in one year just from the sale of his articles. When I told my writer friends about him, they immediately wanted to know his success secret. On rereading his story, we determined that he had mastered the art of delegation. Instead of trying to do everything himself, he had hired a secretary to type his manuscripts and take care of correspondence. He employed two young research assistants who were eager for exposure and an opportunity to develop their skills. Thus, the writer was free to spend his time where he could be most productive. He increased his output and his paycheck.

The late John Cash Penney was once quoted as saying that the wisest decision he ever made was realizing he couldn't do everything by himself. By delegating and getting some help, he was able to develop and create hundreds of stores, giving thousands of employees a chance for work and personal growth.

Henry Ford was a master of delegation. Once he was involved in a lawsuit because someone called him a fool. He explained he was no fool for he had five buttons on his desk. When he didn't know the answer to a question he would push one of those buttons and an expert would walk in to answer that question. He explained he could hire experts very reasonably to make him more effective.

In my work I used to think I had to do everything by myself. As a result I stifled my progress. When I decided to become master of my time rather than its servant, I realized that proper delegation was the best way to increase my productivity.

When planning to delegate, first decide exactly what you should be doing with your time. You can do this by asking questions like, "How can I be most effective? What are my greatest strengths? What unique contributions do I have to make?"

Second, ask, "What am I doing now that could be delegated to someone else?" Don't do anything you can get someone else to do for you. Once you have the answers to those questions, you need a basic understanding of the principles behind delegation.

There is a specific procedure to follow when you ask someone to do something for you.

1. Make sure the person being given the opportunity, job, or task is aware of its relative importance. Allow them to feel your complete trust and respect and let them know how much you are counting on them to succeed.

Sometimes just choosing a proper job title can boost the individual's self-esteem and cause them to take extra pride in their position. My administrative assistant started out with me as a clerk typist. Later she wanted to be referred to as my secretary. I noticed she didn't really like this title either, so I made her my assistant and finally my administrative assistant. My company still has her job listed as clerk typist, but she and I both know better. She is more than a clerk typist in her own self-esteem. The increase in her self-esteem was valuable in making her more productive, responsible, and capable.

2. Arrange for a special orientation meeting to outline the various requirements of the position or task, and provide the individual with the necessary materials and information. This is the time to let the person know exactly what level of performance will be expected.

It is especially important to remember this principle when dealing with our children. Too often we set them up for failure because we neglect to teach and communicate effectively. Sometimes it takes a little ingenuity to get our message across.

One mother wanted her four-year-old daughter to learn how to set the table at dinner time. In order to prepare her and ensure the child's success, they sat down together and pasted a paper replica of how the table should look when it was finished. The child then had a correct model to follow. It is equally important that we provide our employees with the same kind of clear-cut examples to follow.

3. Always work with the end results in mind. Unfortunately, many parents and employers put more focus on the methods rather than on the results. In fact, methods sometimes become the objective. When delegating, don't expect the individual to do it just as you would. They may, in time, learn to do it better.

In my work I let my assistants and associates know what my objectives are and then I encourage them to magnify their own potential by using their own abilities and judgment. As long as the objectives are agreed upon, the person assigned the task should be given as much freedom as possible.

4. Secure a commitment, set a deadline, and follow through. Whether you are dealing with children, co-workers, baby-sitters, or the young man you hire to mow your lawn, there should always be an accounting or follow-through. In the end, you are the one doing the delegating and the one responsible for these people's productivity.

5. Give incentives and rewards commensurate to the work done. Never delegate without such a goal or reward. Adults, of

course, should be paid well for the work they accomplish; generally speaking, the more generous you are with your money, the greater will be your return.

Rewards do not always have to be monetary. A newspaper editor in Atlanta told his department that if everyone completed all their assignments by noon Friday, they could have the afternoon off to do whatever they pleased. To date, every deadline has been met. Because everyone must be finished, there is much more cooperation, encouragement, and helpfulness among employees.

A good way of determining how much you are willing to pay is to decide how important the task is to you. For example, I pay my baby-sitter well for the work she does, because I depend so completely on her for my children's welfare. I must have the best care I can afford for my own peace of mind.

You may decide you would like to have a beautiful garden and a well-manicured lawn. The youngster down the street might be willing to mow your lawn and trim your hedges for a small fee, but you may not get the quality of workmanship desired. If it is really important to you, hire a professional and pay more.

Children also need to be rewarded for their work. Some parents pay money, others use different incentives such as, "When you finish vacuuming, you may go to your friend's house," "If you will help me with the yard work, I will help you make a new dress," "When the dishes are done, you and I can go to the circus."

Initially, delegation takes extra time and involves risks. It takes time to train subordinates and children, and there is a risk because they may not do it as you would. But for most of us, there is a firm reality to deal with: *unless we delegate, we will not have the time to complete our major goals and objectives!*

What should you delegate? Everyone's needs and resource people are different. You might want to consider some of these chores and activities:

Household chores. If trained properly, children can be the best help. The greatest obligation we have to our children is to teach them how to care for themselves when they no longer have us around. If we truly love our children we will not give them everything they ask for. But we can teach them how to utilize their energies for the objects they want. Making objects too easy to obtain only makes your children weak, and they will not know how to meet future needs. Daryl Hoole, in her book *The Art of Teaching Children* (Desert Books, Salt Lake City), has several fine suggestions on this subject.

One word of caution: if you delegate to your spouse, don't expect perfection. Just be grateful for his or her willingness to help.

Errands. I know of one young woman who has a thriving business in her neighborhood running errands for other people. If you don't have such a service nearby, children, high school students, and secretaries are also good at handling details of this type.

Chauffeuring the kids. Again, hire a reliable teenager or college student to chauffeur the kids to their dancing lessons and Little League practice. If one is not available, consider carpooling with other parents.

Keeping abreast of the news. The President has someone read the newspapers and keep him briefed. I know of one young busy mother who decided to try the same thing. She delegated the job to her teenagers, asking them to prepare a one-page news brief every day to be delivered at dinner time. The kids kept up on current events and she was able to use the time for other activities.

I personally do not have the time or the motivation to read the newspaper daily. I used to read it from cover to cover, afraid I'd miss something and appear ignorant of the world's events. For a broadcaster this would be embarrassing. I'd no more than get through the morning paper when the evening paper would arrive. I calculated that I had about an hour every day to get my work done. I was also suffering from reading daily reports of child abuse, rape, murder, inflation, energy shortages, and other negative news. Knowing that every minute you spend with a negative thought takes one hundred minutes to erase made me realize that starting my day with negative programing was not healthy or productive. Now I skim the paper for a general idea of current events and have my assistant circle articles that pertain to areas we're discussing on my television show that she feels I'd be interested in. I'm sure I miss out on a lot, but I'm not sure I'm any worse off. I do catch a few minutes of news on the radio and TV, but manage to combine this with other activities. I find it really takes very little time to keep current, especially if you listen to the topics people are discussing.

Spring cleaning. If you can't afford regular cleaning help, consider hiring a professional service for the big spring-cleaning jobs, or at least hire a neighborhood teenager to help you. You will be giving a teenager an opportunity to learn something and to earn some money.

Giving a party. If possible, hire someone else to do the catering, even if it is just your next-door neighbor who makes terrific lasagna. This will free you to spend more time with the guests and enjoy the party.

Heavy yard work. If you can hire a professional, do it. If not, teenagers may be your best bet. (Or put in a lawn that requires minimal maintenance.)

Laundry. Consider sending shirts or other time-consuming items to the laundry. One woman admitted she had ironed shirts for seven years only to realize the cost of sending them out to be starched and laundered was small compared to the time she saved. If you can afford this expenditure but still need further incentive, consider that clothes will last longer and look better if professionally laundered. Your time will be better spent doing more rewarding things.

In conclusion, remember time is money. If you spend all your time doing the little day-to-day chores that could be delegated to the children or hired out for a small fee, you never will have time to enlarge your career or make that million dollars you have been dreaming about.

Delegation will also give you more time to spend on the things you most enjoy in life. It will teach your children responsibility, and it will give others a chance to develop their talents, skills, and abilities.

I'll never forget hearing someone say, "Failure to delegate is like going out and buying a watchdog, bringing it home, and then doing all the barking yourself."

WE LEARN BY DOING

The only way to learn how to be a tennis champ is by playing the game. We can hear about it, read about it, and watch others play, but until we develop our own skills, we will only be spectators. It is the same with time management. You can read this book and study what other experts have to say on the subject, but until you put the principles into practice for yourself, you will never become the master of your time.

On pages 222 through 225 you will find several exercises designed to help you plan, eliminate the nonessentials, and delegate. If you work consistently in all of these areas, you will begin to find more time to enjoy life, and, most important, you will realize your greatest potential.

5
Letting Your Imagination
Spring to Life

Before you can do something
You must first be something.

—Goethe

If your fairy godmother were suddenly to flash into your home tonight, wave her magic wand, and say, "The daydream is yours. In twenty-four hours you may live out your fantasy!" would you honestly feel prepared for the experience?

It may be difficult to admit where you are on the spectrum in relationship to your overall goal. But self-analysis is necessary if you are to move forward.

One young woman who recently took my workshop told me of the lesson she had learned about personal preparation. She explained: "When I was a young girl I desperately wanted to be Miss America. Every year I faithfully watched the famed pageant on television and as the new queen was chosen and Bert Parks sang his song, I would run to my bedroom mirror, stare at my reflection and whisper, 'Someday you are going to be on that stage and feel that crown being placed on your head.'

"The years passed and I continued to watch the pageant and dream. I sent away for the official Miss America Pageant requirements, talked to girls who had competed in local pageants, and occasionally I tried various diet and exercise programs that might enhance my figure.

"When I finally reached the age to compete I was excited to try out for the local pageant. My desire was still fresh in my memory, and I thought I only had to enter the contest to make it come true. How wrong I was. When I got there I discovered there were girls who had worked harder at perfecting their talents. They had spent more time perfecting their figures, and they had developed more poise and confidence. I went home a loser. But even then I realized I had not lost to anyone but myself. Deep inside of me I still knew I had the potential to be a Miss America. I just hadn't spent enough time turning myself into one. I resolved right then and there that I would never be defeated by myself again."

THE DIFFERENCE BETWEEN DREAMING AND TRAINING

The principle of personal readiness is one of the most important qualifications for turning a daydream or goal into reality. Although visualization and daydreaming can help in our pursuit, they are only effective when coupled with good hard work.

A counselor within a large university recently reported that there was very little competition for high-paying jobs. "Positions that pay well and offer good advancement and plenty of fringe benefits sit in my desk drawer for months," he explained. "Students want the best jobs, but they just aren't willing to turn themselves into the qualified people most companies are seeking."

The Bible teaches that you cannot put new wine in old bottles. So it is with goals and daydreams. You cannot make them true until you have developed the personality, skills, and strengths necessary for the experience.

Recently a young woman came into my workshop with a goal and a problem. Her goal was to get out of debt. Her husband had been making good money as a doctor but had decided to return to school to specialize. His paycheck had been drastically reduced, but the bills from the past were continuing to roll in.

Because her husband would be totally involved and preoccupied with his studies for the next three years, I counseled her to take the initiative to remove those debts.

After checking her previous experience, I was delighted to learn she had the skills to market herself as a teacher, fashion consultant, or seamstress. Although she had several ways to remove the mountain of debt, she still lacked one important tool: the shovel.

The shovel would have to be her personality. Even though she had all the talents and background required for financial success, she just didn't have the confidence or assertiveness to sell herself.

The last time I saw her she admitted to taking a part-time job as a receptionist for $3.10 an hour. It was only a fraction of what she could have made at her other jobs, but until she was willing to develop the personality skills that were lacking, her potential for making money was limited.

Change is never easy. It is often difficult to form new habits and behaviors and sometimes it can be quite frustrating. In a sense, we have to leave our comfort zone. But change is a necessity when we have big goals and dreams. Sometimes we have to lose weight or give up smoking or start jogging. Sometimes we have to learn how to control our tempers or become more adept at expressing our feelings. And sometimes we have to return to school and give up our current jobs in order to prepare for more rewarding financial futures. Whether we have the courage to make these changes and succeed depends a great deal on our own willingness to expand and become better people. Attitude and enthusiasm for the project at hand is always important.

Recently I heard a cute story about a young woman who wanted to catch the eye of a particular young man. She had been noticing him on campus for weeks but had never managed to meet him. She had just about decided to give up, but fortunately a wise friend convinced her she just needed to do a little homework. Her friend suggested she find out five things about the young man: 1) his favorite color, 2) his favorite food, 3) what he liked to do with his leisure time, 4) whether he preferred blondes, brunettes, or redheads, and 5) what he liked to read.

The young woman began doing her homework. From talking with mutual friends, she learned that the fellow's favorite color was green, he loved pecan pie, he liked to go fishing on Saturday mornings, he preferred redheads, and he really enjoyed reading Keats.

The young woman now knew how to proceed. She changed her light-brown hair to an auburn shade, purchased a green blouse, went to the library and brushed up on Keats, and then went home to bake her pecan pie.

The next Saturday morning she actually arose at four, put on her jeans and new green blouse, packed a lunch (complete with pecan pie), tucked in a copy of Keats, and took out her fishing pole. She found a comfortable spot, cast in her line just as he was arriving on the scene. Well, you can imagine what she reeled in that day. Needless to say, it was the beginning of many happy hours spent together.

Take time to review the requirements for your goals and daydreams. Try to become just as specific as this young girl was. If you are trying for a top position with a big company, do a little research. Find out exactly what they are looking for. Know what kind of executives they have hired in the past. Try to become the kind of person they want. If you want to become a better parent to your children, talk with them. Find out what qualities they would most appreciate in you. Do they want you to spend more time with them, or plan more family outings? You don't have to sacrifice your own personality and character in order to add to and improve upon it.

Once you have reviewed your requirements, make a resolution to begin the transformation process. Here are six very positive methods that can help you change into the individual you would most like to become.

Method 1: Setting Yourself Up for Success

Remember your excitement when the Apollo II landed and men actually walked on the moon? It was incredible to realize that a piece of machinery could lift off this planet and travel to a destination so far away.

I am told that when Neil Armstrong was a young boy playing in a sandbox, his mother came outside to get him for lunch. She noticed he had a small toy airplane in his hand. As she approached he said, "Mother, one day I am going to fly to the moon." She said she never doubted it.

Although most of us were impressed with the outer-space part of the voyage, it was the takeoff that required the most energy.

Changing yourself, especially breaking bad habits, is much the same way. It is the blast-off, the breaking away from our old self or the attempt to develop a new skill, that is the most difficult. John Grogan, a consultant in sales techniques, relays the following traditional riddle in his tape "Secrets of Time Management Success" (John Grogan and Associates, P.O. Box 352, Scottsdale, AZ 85252):

I am your constant companion. I am your greatest helper or your heaviest burden. I will push you onward or drag you down to failure. I am at your command. Half of the tasks that you do you may just as well turn over to me and I will do them quickly and correctly. I am easily managed, you must merely be firm with me. Show me exactly how you want something done. After a few lessons I will do it automatically. I am the servant of all great people, and alas, of all failures as well. Those who are great, I have made great. And those who are failures, I have made failures. I am not a machine but I work with all the precision of a machine plus the intelligence of a person. You may run me for profit or run me for ruin, it makes no difference to me. Take me, train me, be firm with me and I will lay the work at your feet. Be easy with me and I will destroy you. Who am I? I am called habit. Habit is my name.

Successful people get into the habit of success. They learn how to have a success experience and then repeat the experience again and again and again. First we must make our habits—then our habits make us.

Unfortunately, most of us are great starters but poor finishers. We start a stringent diet on Monday but fall off the wagon by Wednesday. We resolve to get up earlier to make better use of our time but can't quite seem to get our heads off the pillow the first time we try. Gradually, failure adds to failure, and instead of lifting off the launch pad, we sink deeper and deeper into our frustration, self-pity, and misery. All of this failure could be avoided by simply assessing our real level of competence, and then taking one small step forward. Consider the following example:

A young girl eagerly began piano lessons but soon became disheartened when the teacher asked her to practice one hour each day. After a few abortive attempts, she began complaining to her parents, and within weeks she was begging to quit.

Together the teacher, parents, and child sat down for a consultation. "How much practice time are you willing to put in?" asked the teacher of the child.

The child thought and thought and finally decided she could handle twenty minutes a day, ten minutes in the morning and ten in the afternoon.

The teacher wisely accepted the girl's proposal and cut the previous assignment, requiring the young girl to learn only three simple songs for the following week.

When the child came to the next lesson she was prepared.

The three songs were learned perfectly, and her practice chart showed twenty minutes of real practice time every day.

Gradually the teacher added a little more practice time and a few more songs. Soon the child was learning to compose her own songs. Three years later the little girl was featured as a star performer in the annual recital. She played her own melodies for the audience, heard the applause, and felt like a real musician as she walked off the stage.

But just imagine what would have happened if the teacher had continued to insist on an hour of practice every day. The young girl would have undoubtedly quit, and her talent as a composer would never have been discovered or developed.

Although we as adults are often wise when teaching and training our young children, we tend to let such wisdom fly out the window when dealing with ourselves. We expect to play sonatas after our first piano lesson, hit tennis balls like Chris Evert Lloyd after our first experience on the tennis court, and bake soufflés like Julia Child, when if we have barely learned to boil water.

In the areas you are trying to change or develop, consider what promises you are capable of keeping. If you are trying to give up smoking, ask yourself if you can go for one hour without lighting up. If you are trying to improve your vocabulary, try learning just one new word a day. Never make a promise you can't keep, but always keep the promises you make. Gradually you will get the power to pull away from the negative gravitational force that has stunted your growth for so long.

Method 2: Learn How to Make Positive Choices

In order to succeed with our new habit patterns, we have to learn how to make positive choices when confronted with life's myriad experiences. Although a few social scientists, gurus, and educators will still insist our negative behavior is the result of a subconscious child driving us toward self-destruction, belief that an individual is a free agent is more than positive-thinking rhetoric.

Have you ever considered exactly what the word *choice* means, or how many choices you make every day? Choosing means to pause and stand back for perspective, to think deeply, and then to choose our actions and reactions. It means exercising our freedom, but it also means accepting responsibility for ourselves and our attitudes, and refusing to blame others for circumstances.

I've heard happiness described as making the right choices. Only you can do that for yourself.

Proponents of transactional analysis suggest that we have a "precious moment" in which to choose the way we will react to any outside stimulus. During that crucial moment we can ignore our gift of free agency, or we can allow our minds to click creatively through the dozens of available responses to any condition or stimulus.

Consider the way we respond to the many emotionally packed situations we encounter throughout life. How we handle feelings of jealousy, hurt, anger, rejection, or fright can affect our ability to accomplish and conquer a problem or goal.

Henry Hines, a world-class long jumper and sprinter, tells an amusing story about his response to an ego attack from his younger sister.

It seems that Henry grew up with a sister who was a very achievement-oriented young lady. Every weekend she would come home with all kinds of medals and ribbons for her expertise in track and field, while the older Hines contributed nothing to the family trophy case.

Finally Henry decided to do something about the jealousy he was feeling and challenged his sister to a fifty-yard dash. But instead of proving his superiority, he was beaten, and beaten badly. Says Henry, "It was a pretty low blow to my ego and everybody teased me for weeks afterward."

Put yourself in Henry's "precious moment" of decision and

consider how you would have handled the situation. The young boy might have assumed, because of one loss, that he was athletically inferior. He could have withdrawn from his friends and peers. He might have even decided to hold a lifelong grudge against the one who had made him appear so foolish.

Fortunately, Henry made a wise decision. He responded to the failure by going out for the track team. By the time he was a senior in college, Hines had become an internationally recognized athlete, holding several world records. Many people believe that successful achievers have at some time in their life felt discrimination, inferiority, or severe criticism. Achievement can be the result of turning a negative into a positive.

The very fact that people can and do respond to stressful situations in a positive way helps to reinforce the validity of the idea of free agency.

As a high school senior I was advised not to pursue a college degree. Very gently, a counselor told me I was not college material. She pointed out that I had not taken the necessary preparatory courses and that my family's limited financial resources could not cover further educational costs.

My mother also tried to sway me from college. She stated that a college degree would be a waste of time for a future wife and mother. She explained that once children are in the picture there is no point in pursuing a career. It would be impossible to do both well. I can also remember being told, "Don't try to get above your raising."

My boyfriend, a brilliant engineering student at Vanderbilt University, also felt that college was an impossibility for me. He too pointed out that I had never really been dedicated to academics and that college required a lot of effort and determination.

I could have listened to all the negatives, not making any attempt to better my education. Or I could satisfy my desire to learn more. I stubbornly chose to stick to my desire. In only three years I graduated from Middle Tennessee State University as an honor student with a B.S. degree (normally requiring four years of effort) and married that brilliant Vanderbilt student. I combined marriage, parenthood, and career most successfully by reminding myself of Calvin Coolidge's famous statement

PRESS ON!

Nothing in the world can take the place of persistence. Talent will not: Nothing is more common than unsuccessful men with talent. Genius will not: Unrewarded genius is almost a proverb. Education will not: The world is full of educated derelicts. Persistence and determination alone are omnipotent. The slogan "Press On!" has solved and always will solve the problem of the human race.

Even though none of us lives in a vacuum and even though we do run into unexpected social currents that can toss us off balance or cause us to lose confidence, we have a choice. We can respond positively or negatively to any given situation. We can stay on a diet even when offered a delicious-looking piece of pie from our mother-in-law, or give up smoking even when everyone in the room lights up. If we've made a promise to ourselves to react positively to any negative situation, we must, like Henry Hines, stay on course, even in the face of failure or humiliation. You'll find that discipline in one area makes it easier to be disciplined in other areas. Consider, for example, the hard-working, dedicated athletes who spend hundreds of hours training to perfect their skill; it is impressive to a prospective employer to realize a person is capable of such hard work, dedication, and discipline.

Method 3: Make Your Honor Greater than Your Mood

Social situations can destroy personal resolutions but so can a bad thought or mood. In order to successfully change yourself, you must learn how to control your mind—to stamp out a bad thought, a feeling of discouragement, or a desire to quit and give up. Sound impossible? It isn't. I know of many successful people who claim that the ability to control their thoughts and needs is the only thing that has allowed them to come out on top in any situation.

Perhaps your goal is to stay on a diet long enough to lose twenty pounds. You have great success for ten days but then a setback arises. On the eleventh morning you step on the scales to discover you haven't dropped an ounce for the past four days. You've tried so hard. You've stuck with the prescribed program perfectly, but now discouragement has opened a wedge in your armor against the will of your appetite. As you prepare for the day, a dozen alternatives and images race through your mind.

"Give up!" says one voice. "Give yourself a treat. There are always plenty of other diets to try next week."

"Maybe you're not capable of losing weight," says another voice. "Why not quit trying and just accept your body the way it is?"

Another voice says, "I'm angry. Everyone told me this diet would work, but it didn't. Just to show them, I'm going to go out and stuff myself!"

Now stop right there for one moment. Calm the voices inside your head and repeat out loud, *"That was an interesting thought, but it was just a thought. I love myself too much to quit or fail. I will do something to help myself succeed."*

Then go out and do something positive for yourself. Consider spending a day at Elizabeth Arden's or going for a hard workout at the spa. Curl up with an exciting mystery novel, go for a long walk, or plant a garden, but don't let yourself give in to the negative thoughts, because they will destroy your resolve and your chances for future success. Let me repeat, for every minute spent thinking negatively, it takes one hundred minutes to erase that negativity.

Method 4: Add Staying Power with Visualization

A world-renowned concert pianist once admitted his dislike of practicing. He had studied the instrument for only seven years before embarking upon his career, and he seldom sat down at the keyboard for any length of time. When an interviewer questioned him about the unusually small amount of time devoted to the instrument, he replied, "I practice in my head."

We can achieve much through "practicing in our heads." In fact, when we combine positive visualization with hard work we can almost always guarantee success. It must, however, be combined with work.

I once heard of a young man paralyzed in an automobile accident. He asked his nurse to place a chart with typing symbols over his bed. She asked him whether he could type and he said no, but he had always wanted to learn. He studied that chart for months while undergoing therapy to regain use of his arms. Later he asked another nurse to bring in a typewriter so he could write a letter. She had no idea he had never typed before, but immediately filled his request. He asked her to time his speed. On his first physical attempt at typing he was able to type almost thirty-eight words per minute without errors. Notice I said *physical* attempt. Mentally he had been typing for months. He had visualized his index finger touching certain keys, the placement of his hands on the home row, the necessary thumb action, and so forth. His fingers had practiced mentally through visualization long before he had actually touched a typewriter.

Another case I heard about was that of a promising golfer who was drafted and sent to Vietnam just at the time he was to compete for the pro tour. Friends thought his military obligation would hurt his golfing abilities. He too became concerned at not having the opportunity to practice, but he wanted to be able to compete once again when he got out of the service. Every day he mentally practiced his putting and driving to keep his skills sharpened. When he got out of the service and shot his first round of golf, he was amazed at how he had improved. Friends couldn't believe it either. He easily qualified for the pro golf tour. He actually had never stopped practicing his golf. Visualization had made it possible for him to continue and even improve his game.

Real visualization isn't just daydreaming, it is picturing and imagining precisely how we wish to act or react to a future event. It is the creative use of the right side of your brain. Runners sometime spend a half hour picturing themselves in a race before they actually go out to compete. I know of a very successful businessman who will spend a few minutes visualizing his success before he ever goes to talk to an important client. Successful people always imagine what they want to happen. They store many positive experiences in their subconscious. Unsuccessful people only visualize and imagine what they don't want to happen. Thus, they have no previous success record to rely on when they are called upon to perform.

Before I get out of bed in the morning on the day I have a seminar, workshop, speech, or television taping, I imagine myself delivering the presentation exactly the way I want it to be. This is a very important way of practicing my delivery. I see the audience's reaction and hear their applause. I see myself concluding with a feeling of satisfaction.

I also lie in bed a few moments longer and visualize a perfect, sound body with no aches or pains. I feel energy and strength flowing through my entire system. I promise myself that I'm going to have a happy, productive day. Isn't it amazing how we manifest our expectations—good or bad.

You can use positive visualization to help yourself in many ways. You can change a poor attitude, improve your self-image, increase motivation, and in general overcome the limitations imposed by yourself and others.

Whenever I feel shy or insecure in a social setting, I visualize how my friend Daisy would act under similar conditions. She is more outgoing, personable, and enthusiastic in a crowd of strangers than I. I hear myself greeting strangers the same way she would and asking similar interesting questions to break the ice and stimulate conversation. No one who has seen me do this would ever believe I am the least bit shy. I've always been an advocate of being yourself or you'll mess up trying to be someone else, but there are occasions when adopting the characteristics of someone you admire can improve your behavior.

I also use this visualization technique when I have a tough or controversial interview on my television show. I visualize that I am Barbara Walters, whose interviewing skills I admire greatly. I visualize her conducting the interview. I am amazed at how well I do — or I guess I should say, how well Barbara does!

Recently I read of a man who had been a steady smoker for thirty years. He smoked twenty to thirty cigarettes a day. One day he woke up to realize he was not enjoying the experience. He didn't try to quit immediately but started taking a few notes. How many of the cigarettes did he actually enjoy? The answers varied, but usually he liked only two or three, and then only the first one or two puffs.

He decided to visualize himself not liking cigarettes at all. After about six weeks he found his self-image changing. He went from "I am a smoker," to "I am a nonsmoker." Within three months he broke his addiction to cigarettes forever.

We act as our self-image demands. If we want to change our behavior, we must first work on changing our self-image. Perhaps you are not an assertive person and lack the courage to stand up for yourself. Rather than working specifically on your behavior, you could start working on your image. Spend time visualizing yourself as an assertive individual. Imagine all the situations that might occur where you could demonstrate your assertiveness. If you practice this technique on a daily basis, you will gradually find yourself acting assertive with almost no conscious effort.

Truly positive visualization is one of the most powerful tools we have to help us make the changes we desire. Research is just beginning to tap the beneficial effects it can have on each person's performance, behavior, and even health. I feel that the future treatment of disease and illness will use more and more of this type of therapy. There has been too much positive research to ignore its potential in the healing process.

Method 5: Getting Help from the Experts

As we discussed in Chapter 3, it is imperative to have good role models when we attempt to achieve a goal or a dream. Even though role models may not have accomplished exactly what we hope to, they can still help to pull us through the hard times. They can be especially helpful when we are trying to change and improve ourselves.

Recently I spoke with a man who had achieved great success selling automobiles. He had come to Arizona with absolutely nothing, and yet he had become one of the most successful businessmen in Phoenix. I asked him how he did it. He explained, "When I first started in the automobile business I was impressed and even awed by some of the people I had contact with. They were either employers or people involved in some way with the business. My first impressions were that it would be almost impossible to duplicate their accomplishments. I just couldn't believe I could ever do what they were doing, earn what they were earning, or be involved as they were.

"However, I continued to study these people. I took in their activities and tried to picture myself doing what they did by comparing my way with theirs. Over a period of time I found myself believing I could do certain things as well as they were doing them, and I seized every opportunity to prove my ability.

"When I found I could do one part of their job as well as they did, I felt I could do other parts equally well. Systematically I built up my confidence. I found it was a simple matter of reducing the whole into small parts, and in this manner I was able to reach my goal and incorporate their values and abilities into my own character."

In my workshops I have advised participants to think of

someone who has already accomplished a similar goal, and then keep that person in mind at all times. I have had many reports of personal success as a result. One young woman told me she was able to stay on her diet because she always imagined her Weight Watcher lecturer was helping her prepare and eat every meal. Another woman said that she was able to discipline herself to write every day because she imagined Erma Bombeck sitting in her home doing the same thing. I even know of a woman who said she had a successful pregnancy because she kept imagining her friend who had recently had twins. She said, "If that woman can make it through twins, then certainly I can make it through the delivery of one child." And of course, she did.

Seek out the top authority in the field in which you desire to excel. You'll be amazed at how eager successful people are to share the secrets of their success. People become rich by enriching others. They got where they are by helping other people. They will be willing to give you advice as well.

Method 6: The Ultimate Commitment

Thus far we have discussed many successful ways to help ourselves change, but by far the best method of all is commitment—total commitment. We can achieve almost anything we set out to accomplish, if we have made the right kind of commitment.

Commitment builds enthusiasm and forces us to use our creativity. Commitment prevents ultimate failure, because commitment does not allow us to quit. Miracles can and do occur with the right kind of commitment. I know of a man who had previously failed the law school entrance exam three times but finally passed it and made it into law school. Without the commitment he had made to become a lawyer, he is sure he would never have persisted. Billie Jean King made a commitment to become a great tennis champion when she was one hundred pounds overweight and wore thick bifocals, yet she managed to achieve her goal. I know of others who have come through accidents, losses, and other kinds of experiences that would have caused all but the most valiant to give up, yet because of their determination and commitment, they went on to achieve great success.

It is important to make the right kinds of commitments, however. We need different types of commitments for different types of situations. A commitment that starts with "I will never . . . " may work well for the individual trying to give up smoking but lead to an ultimate failure for the individual trying to stick with a diet. Sometimes it is better to say, "No matter what happens . . . I will not give up in my quest." That gives us room and flexibility, but still assures us of success.

When making a commitment, it is important to remember the spirit as well as the letter of our intent. What if you were committed to studying every day for two hours until you finished your degree. Would that ensure your success? Sitting at a desk with an open book does not guarantee that any knowledge will seep into our brains. However, if we make that two-hour study commitment and attempt to keep the spirit—that is, try to learn something—we have a pretty good chance of succeeding.

Once again, remember that commitment—total commitment to a change—is the greatest guarantee we have for future success. It is one of the most important aspects in achieving our goals and making our dreams come true.

NOW IS THE TIME TO START

You now have six really terrific ways to change or improve any element of your character or physical make-up you desire, but none of the methods will work without your personal enthusiasm and dedication.

Goethe wrote, "Lose this day loitering, 't will be the same

story tomorrow and the next more dilatory. Indecision brings its own delays and days are lost lamenting over days. Action—there is courage, magic in it. Once started, the mind grows heated. Begin the job and the world will be completed."

THOUGHT PRECEDES ENERGY?

The best time to start making changes is right now. Don't wait until next month or even next Monday. Begin this day, this hour, this minute. Change starts by taking action—positive action. In your workbook section (pages 226 through 228) you will find several exercises to help you get started.

Let Your Environment Work for You

We shape our houses, then our houses shape us.
—Winston Churchill

Does your environment reflect you? Is it your style? Is it the kind of place that allows you to bloom to your fullest potential, or does it stifle you and get in the way of your success?

To answer that question, I'd like you to play the "private-eye game." Pretend you are a detective and snoop around your house as if you were a stranger trying to find out about the person who lives there. Open the closets, the cabinets, and the drawers. Take a peek inside the refrigerator and oven. Analyze the furniture, the rugs, the draperies, and the pictures on the wall. Study the general state of clutter and/or order. Consider the arrangement of space, the lighting, and the color schemes. How does this environment make you feel? Complete your inventory, then answer the following questions:

1. Would this person waste a lot of time hunting for the things he/she needs?
2. Are his/her tools, equipment, and supplies stored near the work area?

3. Is his/her most frequently used equipment placed beyond reach, making it difficult to grasp items quickly?
4. Does he/she have too many tools cluttering available work space or getting in the way?
5. Would he/she have a tendency to put off doing chores or jobs because he/she lacked the necessary supplies and equipment?
6. Is any of his/her equipment in need of repair or not suited for the job for which it is intended?
7. Can he/she relax in this environment?
8. Is the lighting conducive to his/her success, or might it possibly cause eye strain?

When it comes to success, the design and organization of our environment will either help or hinder us. The answers to the questionnaire and the results of your snooping might have come as a pleasant surprise ("Hey, I really like my home and surroundings. I am actually a pretty organized person!") or as a shock to your psyche ("Am I really that messy and disorganized? I don't know if the person I see living in this environment is the person I really want to be!").

One of the first things I usually tell anyone who is trying to change or improve his lot in life is to begin by changing and improving his environment. I don't mean you should immediately go out and buy a lot of status symbols that will impress the neighbors, nor do I mean you should invest in a $200,000 house if the mortgage payments will send you to the poor house. I mean that slowly, piece by piece, step by step, you should begin organizing and improving your environment until it is a place that allows you to function in comfort and at a level of peak productivity. Improved surroundings improve one's consciousness. Live in the best surroundings: improve your home; drive the best car you can afford; and always dress with finesse—even smell your best. All of these will help raise your consciousness. Once your consciousness is raised you will notice an improvement in your life. You will become more aware and soon find that success has become a habit. Your best environment will be one that positively affects and reflects you. It may be a mansion in Beverly Hills, a farmhouse in Vermont, or a little apartment in lower Manhattan. It may contain a large study and library or a deluxe kitchen with every convenience and gadget known to humankind. However, if it isn't clean, organized, and totally effective in meeting your specific needs, it will never bring you the satisfaction you desire. Although dream homes take time to build and create, you can begin to improve your environment now—whatever your situation. Making the most of what you have right now is what this chapter is all about.

THE BUG LIST

In my workshops I always tell participants to start on their home and office improvement by making a general "Bug List." In other words, what changes could you be making today that would allow you to be more successful tomorrow, or what bugs you the most about your current environment? Is it the color of paint on the walls? The closet you avoid opening because it's filled to overflowing? The lack of plants or pretty accessories? Perhaps you feel frustrated because your kitchen isn't well stocked, or the faucet drips, or because you can never find a pencil when you need one.

I have included two sample bug lists—one made by a single career woman sharing a house with two other women, the other made by a busy homemaker with three young children. Notice how many of their items are actually rather small—things that could be taken care of or improved with just a few hours of work or a trip to the store. You might also analyze how many of the problems are of the women's own making, and how many are simply inherent to the structure of their homes.

BUG LIST (Single Woman's)

I really feel I could function more effectively and comfortably in my environment if:

- My drawers and closets weren't always a mess
- There weren't a perpetual mess on top of the refrigerator
- I could find a sharp knife for cutting when I need one
- We had a different color scheme for the shower curtains and other bathroom accessories
- I could find a pencil by the phone when I need one
- I had an automatic answering service to take my calls when I'm away
- I didn't feel generally embarrassed by the state of my home when company comes
- I could look out at the garden and see something besides weeds
- The garbage cans were bigger

BUG LIST (Married Woman's)

I'm sure I would function more successfully if:

- I didn't have to stand on our water bed in order to see myself full length in the dresser mirror
- I didn't have to run several miles in order to prepare a meal in our country-style kitchen
- I had a self-cleaning oven
- My freshly ironed clothes didn't immediately become wrinkled from being stuffed in my overflowing closets
- I didn't have to stare at my husband's prize hunting trophy when I went to bed at night. I'd also like to get rid of the rug shampooer that has to stand next to our bed because of a general lack of closet space
- I had a magazine rack in the bathroom

- I didn't have to listen to dripping faucets and squeaky doors late at night
- They'd invent an aesthetically pleasing smoke alarm—ours stands out like a sore thumb
- I didn't have to write telephone messages in crayon
- I didn't have to share this single-family dwelling with half of the kids in the neighborhood

You might have found some humor in reading over the items mentioned on the list, but how many similar problems do you have to cope with in your home? On page 231 of your workbook section you will find your own "Bug List" to fill out. The results of this assignment should lead directly to our next area of discussion, "The Procrastination List."

THE PROCRASTINATION LIST

Your procrastination list should include some of the items that appear on your "Bug List" (the ones that are within your financial ability to change or improve) as well as those little items you've been procrastinating about for months. These might include going through your wardrobe to mend, repair, or get rid of outdated items, organizing your kitchen cupboards, cleaning out your garage, getting the backyard in shape, or painting the living room.

As you go down your list (see page 232 of your workbook) to decide which item to work on first, try and analyze the major reasons you've been procrastinating about each task. Perhaps you lack the necessary supplies and equipment to handle the job. If this is the case, purchasing these items should then become one of your highest priorities. Or perhaps you have all the necessary tools and supplies, but the task itself seems too overwhelming or distasteful. You can solve this problem by breaking the task down into small bite-sized chunks, doing one small chore a day, or by challenging yourself to work ten minutes on a project (getting started is the hardest part), or by planning something nice to reward yourself with when the tasks are completed. Of course it may take longer this way, but it's a lot better to proceed in such a systematic manner than to procrastinate indefinitely. This is referred to by many time-management experts as the Swiss-cheese method—putting holes in overwhelming tasks, or visualizing the necessity of having to eat an elephant. You could if you had to, if you did it bite by bite.

ORGANIZING YOUR ENVIRONMENT FOR SUCCESS

No matter what kind of house or apartment you live in, I'll bet if you would let me spend one half hour in it I could show you a way to organize it better—a way that would allow you greater success. Unfortunately, many homes don't even have the basics. Let's discuss some of these:

The Home Office

You deserve an office and you need one because you are an executive in your home. As such, you need a specific place to plan and organize. Invest in a large desk and some files and add some office supplies as your needs and budget allow.

Where to put it? You might turn an extra-large closet into an office, build one under the staircase, create one in your kitchen, or use one of your spare bedrooms. I've turned my beautiful, spacious dining room (that I always dreamed of having for elegant dinner parties) into my work area for this particular book. Right now the book is a high priority, and completing it precludes my being able to entertain for several months. Since my work schedule, combined with family obligations, makes formal entertaining impractical right now, I felt the dining room was currently a wasted space and would be more useful serving as my home office.

If you look around your own home I'm sure you'll find some area that you could stake out as your own place for work—even if it is only to accommodate a particular project temporarily. Boards covered with contact paper placed on top of concrete blocks can be a makeshift solution—and an example of how innovative you can be if you need an office area badly enough.

Michael Vance, who gives a seminar around the country entitled "Adventure in Creative Thinking," advises his students to create an attractively decorated "head room" as a special place to go to for creative thought. Eventually one becomes accustomed to this room or special place as the location that stimulates creative ideas. (For more information on Michael Vance's workshop, write to him at 1010 Palm Avenue, Los Angeles, CA 90069.)

I suggest stocking your home office with the following supplies:

A desk lamp or overhead hanging lamp
A filing cabinet—legal size is best
Manila folders
Scotch tape and masking tape
Rubber bands of all sizes
Scissors
Memo spindle
Paper clips
A roll of stamps
Typewriter
Typing paper, carbons, and second sheets
Pencil sharpener
Ruler
Pencils—at least three dozen

Colored pens
Black ink pen (good for signing letters, etc.)
Postcards
Large wastebasket
Personal stationery with your name and address printed on
    it
Correction fluid
Business cards (optional but highly recommended)
Phone extension with long cord
Calendar
Stapler

Many people ask me just what they should do in their office if they are unaccustomed to using one. I think the office is a great place to plan your menus for the week (if you haven't been subscribing to this practice I guarantee it will save you time), organize the household chores, keep up on correspondence, do any homework you may bring home from the office, and pay and sort bills; and if nothing else, it can be a place to get away from the kids. If you are a homemaker it will help you feel like you're a real executive instead of just a Mommy on twenty-four-hour call. It is the obvious place to work on that book that every person has inside him.

Starting your filing system.   I could not function without my files, and once you've developed some files to fit your personal needs and life-style, you too will wonder how you ever got along without them. If you're starting from scratch, I suggest you gather up all the loose papers floating around your house, as well as important documents such as wills, deeds, mortgage papers, and insurance policies (you may want to keep additional copies of these in your safe-deposit box) and set aside an initial block of time for sorting them. Think of the largest general category that will convey what is inside the folder. Most people make their categories too narrow. (Don't subdivide until it takes more than five minutes to find what you want in the folder.) At this point, you might choose a subheading such as "Childrens' Records and Remembrances," with the subheading "Susie's Art Work." It is better to have only a few fat files than many complicated small ones.

Once you've got your folders ready, discipline yourself to handle each bill, letter, new recipe, washing instruction, or coupon only once. This means you will have to act on an item, file it, or toss it out. This will force you to make an immediate decision, but it will also help you use more of that big round file—the wastebasket!

The Communication Center

A message or communication center will save you hours of time, frustration, and grief. It's a place to leave a note for Johnny, to remind your husband that you still love him even though dinner's going to be late, and it's a good place to jot down phone messages, grocery lists, and little reminders (which should later be transcribed into your Day Timer or appointment book.)

To create your message center I suggest you purchase a large corkboard (the larger your family, the larger your corkboard), a large yearly calendar with plenty of space to write on each day (although you may use your Day Timer, your family still needs to see what's going on), plenty of push pins, a pencil with a string attached that can be permanently tacked to the board, and a supply of note paper for phone messages. You might also want to post a list of emergency phone numbers and phone numbers you most often call, the weekly menu, a list for noting needed grocery items, and your tentative schedule for getting the housework done (this is also a good place to post the children's chore assignments). Hang the board near the phone, and encourage everyone to use it.

The Household Instruction Booklet

The household instruction booklet is for the kids, your spouse (in case you have to be gone for any length of time), the baby sitter, the house sitter, or anyone else who may need help in running your home. Include a list of emergency phone numbers (the veterinarian, the hospital, the fire department, the police, the plumber, the next-door neighbor, the grandparents, the bishop or pastor), instructions for using all major appliances (and whom to call should they go on the blink), and an agenda of the things that usually occur during each day of the week, for example: paper boy collects on Wednesday, the milkman delivers on Mondays, Susie goes for her piano lesson Thursday. I also recommend that you include a presigned emergency release form for a local hospital, in case a child is injured and needs immediate medical attention.

Stocking Your Car

I suggest that you stock your car with the essentials so that you control it, it doesn't control you. Begin by having four sets of keys made and placing them in convenient places around your house and in your purse or billfold. Save one to hide under your car (you can do this with a magnetic key case). If you've ever spent a half hour looking for your keys or have locked your keys in your car, you'll know this is a good time-saving measure.

Clean out your glove compartment and stock it with an address book, a roll of dimes, tissues, a roll of stamps, a package of baby wipes, a pencil, a flashlight, a few Band-Aids, some matches, postcards, small scissors, business cards, a screwdriver, and some note paper (for those flashes of inspiration that always seem to come while driving).

If you have children, I suggest you also make a box of essentials for them. Depending on your children's ages and needs, you might include diapers, diaper wipes, pins, an extra bottle, a can of formula, a few travel games, and perhaps a box or two of animal crackers. If you're going on a longer trip, I suggest you buy several small presents for the children to open, one every hundred miles or so. New toys always keep their attention longer.

I also suggest that you thoroughly clean your car and get it into tiptop repair. Your car controls you if it breaks down. Keep the phone number of the auto club handy with your other numbers and addresses.

Organizing Closet and Shelf Space

One very clever idea for organizing all the cupboards and closets in every room of your house is to analyze each of your storage spaces, giving a 1 to the most convenient, easy-to-reach areas, and a 10 to those places you have to stand on a stepladder, stoop over, or climb over things to reach. Now go through all of your stored items and rate each from 1 to 10. For example, 1s would be things like your everyday china and silverware and your most often used kitchen utensils, whereas a 10 would be that turkey platter you only get out on Thanksgiving, or that cute little Easter bunny you use as a centerpiece in the spring. Everything else gets a number somewhere in between. After you've assigned numbers, simply store number 1 items in number 1 spaces, and so on. Where possible, particularly in your main working areas like the kitchen, sewing room, or office, try to have tools and other utensils within easy reach of your fingertips.

What do you do if you have too many number 1 items and not enough convenient number 1 storage space? I suggest you make a rough sketch of your room and possible storage space, including all unused space such as walls that might hold a pegboard, or cupboards under which you might hang an inconspicuous shelf. If you want to do a little carpentry work to add new cupboards or other storage spaces, you can find many clever ideas in magazines or in the do-it-yourself booklets sold at your local grocery store.

THE ART OF STREAMLINING—
LESS IS MORE

I'm a big believer in getting rid of the clutter and streamlining an environment down to the basic essentials. A certain peace comes with a beautifully streamlined environment, and I challenge you to achieve a similar result in your home. To start with, put away any item that detracts from the style and furnishing of your home. Keep all those bottles and boxes out of sight. If it isn't pretty and attractive, it belongs in a cupboard.

Second, throw away, give away, or sell any items that you don't really need now and probably won't be needing in the future. As Peg Bracken says, "When in doubt—throw it out." I like to ask myself three questions when I'm sorting my possessions:

1. Have I used this item in the past year?
2. Does this object have any monetary, sentimental, or aesthetic value to me?
3. Might this item come in handy someday? If so, when?

A few years ago I decided to tackle boldly the job of cleaning out all my closets and drawers, starting with the clothes closet. Because I hadn't changed dress sizes since high school, I had gotten into the habit of saving many of my favorite old clothes. But rather than enhancing my wardrobe and meeting my current needs, they really tended to hang unworn and take up much valuable closet space.

Because I couldn't afford to go out and buy a new wardrobe, I decided to hold the "First Annual Davenport Boutique Sale."

Since current fashions were longer and I hadn't gotten any shorter, I sent postcards to all my shorter friends, told them to bring their short friends, made up a few refreshments, put out a few of my cookbooks to sell, and prepared for an onslaught of eager buyers. I had put a price tag on everything I owned, including all my shoes, handbags, wigs, scarves, and costume jewelry. When the day was over I had sold literally everything but an old madras blouse left over from college (and in need of a button) and a favorite wraparound skirt not worn for years (for it too needed mending). However, I was $840 richer and I was able to buy an all-new, all-coordinated wardrobe— designed especially to meet the needs of my present life-style. A second payoff was that finally I had an empty closet all to myself. That gave me a real sense of power.

This experience taught me two valuable lessons:

1. What is old to you might be new and valuable to someone else. Rather than trying to recycle old things to fit a new life-style, it's sometimes better to let someone else enjoy them, giving you a chance and an excuse to start fresh and express your current taste.
2. The very idea of starting fresh with new clothes or even new kitchen towels can be very invigorating and give you a feeling of progress. It's a good way to get out of an old rut.

Handbags, Pockets, and Briefcases

In my seminars I offer a prize to the woman who can remove the most unnecessary items from her handbag. It's amazing to see what is carried around that will never come in handy. I feel that no woman can ever be successful in a profession until she can pare down the contents of her purse to the very minimum essentials. Men also should take a critical look at any unnecessary clutter in pockets or briefcases.

KEEPING YOUR HOUSE CLEAN—
DUST IS NOT MOLD

Now that you've organized and streamlined your environment, it's time to talk a little bit about general upkeep and cleanliness. Housework is something we all love to hate. We complain about it, we avoid it and we suffer through it. Very few people learn to love it. It is, however, a task that cannot be ignored.

Have you ever stopped to wonder why it is so hated? Probably because it is done day in and day out, crammed between office jobs or errands, with no relief in sight. It is also mundane and has no immediate reward. There are several approaches to the problem. For example, you can spend one month a year doing a heavy spring cleaning, or you can work out a system of thoroughly cleaning one room a month. The first way is a little overwhelming but it does give you a rather nice feeling at the end. The second way means you have some big cleaning jobs to do every month, but it only has to take a few minutes out of each day.

I know of one woman who decided to get the whole thing over with once a year. Rather than try to tackle the total project herself, she involved her children. To encourage enthusiasm, she suggested they plan a big party to celebrate the end of all their work. Each of the children would be allowed to invite a few of their friends and afterwards the whole family would select a gift to add to the house. To keep momentum and energy high during the month, she played everyone's favorite records on the stereo and served special treats at the end of each cleaning session. By the end of the month my friend had her spring cleaning done, the family had enjoyed a party, and the house had a new addition—a pool table. You might want to try a similar idea with your family.

Once the general cleaning is out of the way, however, you have to analyze what it will require to keep your house in order the other eleven months of the year. I suggest you start by defining the level of cleanliness and order you feel most comfortable with, and then determine what it will take to keep it that way. If you feel a need to have your floors vacuumed daily and the bathrooms scrubbed religiously, you're simply going to have to put in more time than the woman who can function in a more casual atmosphere. Be honest with yourself. Is your current goal more valuable than a spotless house? I doubt that you would be more impressed with Madame Curie for being a spotless housekeeper than for discovering radium. Few successful women can boast about a spotlessly clean house, kept that way by their own energy, and about a successful career as well. And who would pay to attend my seminars or watch my television show if my credentials consisted of my being an excellent housekeeper? We have to admit how little value is placed on such an accomplishment and how little reward one receives for the effort.

When I'm involved in working on a book or a lecture or on producing my show, I sometimes jokingly remind myself that *dust is not mold.* Once you've analyzed what it will take for peace of mind regarding the condition of your home, break the work down into a series of jobs, assign them to responsible family members, and then set a goal to have the housework completed by a certain time each day. Daryl Hoole points out in her frequent lectures on home management, "It takes only five minutes for a five-year-old to make his bed before breakfast, but it may take two hours to get the task completed after he's eaten." She keeps her children honest about finishing their chores by requiring them to have them done before they leave for school in the morning. If one of the kids manages to slip out of the house without doing his work, she will go to school, take him out of class, make him come home and complete his task, and then let him walk back to school alone. She says she's only had to do it twice in the past ten years and it certainly saved her a lot of headaches and frustration. That child has learned to take his mother seriously.

Another woman who has three preschoolers tries to spend five minutes every morning in each room picking items up and straightening out before she starts the major tasks of the day. She can then work in peace without feeling overwhelmed by general untidyness. I'm convinced that these women are successful because they both employ a system tailored to the needs of their family and life-style. They are also consistent in disciplining themselves and making sure other family members carry out their specific responsibilities. Try to apply the same principles to your housework and see how much time you save.

YOUR PERFECT ENVIRONMENT—AN OVERVIEW OF THE BASICS

We've talked about creating perfect environments both in general and in detail. But whether we're talking about the physical structure of your home, the organization, or the cleanliness, I like to channel my thinking into three major categories.

1. **The basics.** Think about the things you can't live without. If you're talking about the house itself, it may be a desire to have your own creative work space, or a big walk-in closet and dressing room, or a double garage. If you're thinking in terms of cleanliness, it may mean you can't function unless the bathroom is sparkling or the dirty dishes are always cleaned away, or the floors are clean and polished. Everyone has their own specific needs. Try and identify yours.

2. **The optional-but-highly-desirables.** Do you want a microwave oven? A swimming pool? A house heated and cooled with solar energy? A new dining-room set? A new car? An airplane? These are the items that may take a little work to achieve but are generally attainable. Keep them in your game plan and work consistently towards them. To keep yourself

constantly reminded, cut out the colored pictures depicting your daydreams, as mentioned earlier, and keep them in a folder. Every once in a while take the folder out and rekindle your desire.

3. The real extravagances. These are items that sometimes seem more like fantasies than real-life possibilities, but they're still attainable. They just take more work. Perhaps yours might include building your own riding stables, owning an expensive original work of art, or having your own exercise room. Or they might be lesser extravagances. One woman said she wished she could have fresh flowers in her house year round but considered it a little beyond her budget at this time. I'm not suggesting you shouldn't have the frills. After all, I dreamed about owning a house that would make Scarlett O'Hara's look like a tract house. I worked hard, and I got it, but it wasn't the first house I owned, and I got the basics before I ever got the extras. By dividing your ideal environment into categories, you can begin to set your priorities and understand what you really need to be happy and successful. Working on the basics also allows you to start improving your situation today. For example, you might not be able to purchase that original Rembrandt this week, but you can clean out a closet that's been driving you crazy, or put a new coat of paint on your bathroom walls, or even buy a new lamp to improve your lighting system. The same applies to your mode of transportation. If you can't afford to buy a Rolls Royce with a portable bar and television, you can at least try to clean out your old VW and stock it with the essentials.

Page 233 of your workbook section is entitled "Environmental Improvements" and contains three columns: "Date," "What I Accomplished," and "How I Felt." Turn to this page, note today's date, challenge yourself to a task you've been putting off, and then describe your success feelings. I guarantee you will begin to feel one hundred percent better about yourself and your surroundings.

DON'T GIVE UP—SHAPE UP!

Someone once said, "Perfection is a process—not an event." I occasionally meet people in my workshops who carry the attitude, "I'm not going to do anything to improve my environment until I can afford my own home, or until I can build my dream house." So they build castles in the air while the dirty dishes pile up in the sink, the closets fill to overflowing, and the termites set up permanent housekeeping. Don't give up your beautiful dreams of the future, but challenge yourself to live in the present. Take a look at what you've got, be grateful it's not less, and then begin taking small, reachable steps to make it better.

The problem most working women face is that they do not have a good wife to come home to. In every culture I know of, married women are mainly responsible for the care and upkeep of the home. I've often joked that even if a woman is a doctor, attorney, or judge, if she's married she is still responsible for washing her husband's socks and underwear.

With economics trends in our country leading more and more women to work outside the home, it is necessary for family members at last to pitch in and do their share of the housework. It is estimated that by 1985 only one out of five women will be financially secure enough to be able to stay home and not work at an outside job. It will be impossible for women to continue to assume all the responsibility for housework while earning money for essentials, without suffering serious effects on their health and well-being.

Families must sit down and look at this situation objectively. Mom is no longer home all day with time to meet the needs of each family member.

THE KEY TO HOUSEHOLD
HEALTH—SIMPLICITY

Simplify your life and keep it that way. Don't let your household control you. Here are a few ideas that I've found useful:

- Clear out one cupboard, drawer, or closet a day until you've organized everything, especially the areas that are bugging you. One a day is not overwhelming.
- Place the most often used items at the front of shelves or cabinets.
- Organize storage areas for items in rooms they are to be used in: sheets in bedrooms, toilet paper in the bathroom, glasses in the bar.
- Have a box for items you know will no longer be used. Place items in the box until the box is filled. Immediately send it to your favorite charity before you have second thoughts.
- Never go to bed without washing dishes and picking up articles such as newspapers, magazines, toys.
- Invest in equipment that is self-cleaning, frost-free, and generally time-saving.
- Have plastic covers on kitchen or dining-room chairs if you have small children.
- Line all trash cans.
- Rinse or wash all dishes immediately. This will eliminate hard to remove stains.
- If your house is large or if you have two floors, have two sets of cleaning equipment. This saves the energy of walking back and forth, up and down.
- Keep loose change in the kitchen for the postman, ice cream man, and so on.
- Buy easy-to-maintain clothes.
- Prepare a handy sewing basket for repairs. Set aside some time every couple of weeks to work on mending.

- Invest in an easy-to-carry basket that will hold all cleaning supplies.
- Use comforters and quilts instead of hard-to-make bedclothes, especially in children's rooms. Encourage children to make their own beds as soon as possible even if the results aren't exactly perfect. (They'll learn if they are given the opportunity, sprinkled with lots of praise and encouragement.)
- If your family prefers cloth napkins, buy each one a different color in a no-iron fabric. They usually last through several meals before needing to be washed.
- Keep the bathtub clean by frequent use of bubble bath. Warn family members not to use too much. It's costly and can be irritating to the skin.
- Keep cleaner under the bathroom and kitchen sinks and make it mandatory that the sink should be cleaned immediately after it has been used.
- If you have several small children, assign each child a color and then make a dot (with magic marker) on each child's clothes. This will make clothes easier to sort after washing.

There are many books that can give you great advice on housekeeping. If you need help, go to an expert. You will find that they have all developed habits of organizing and cleaning on a consistent basis. Parkinson's Law says that work fills the amount of time available. Do the best you can with the amount of time you have. Always remember, "dust is not mold." Whom are you impressed with just because they keep a clean house?

The best housework resource book I've found is entitled *Is There Life After Housework*, by Don Aslett (Reader's Digest Books, New York). He also presents a fascinating, fast-paced, humorous workshop on housekeeping that informs as well as entertains. Don was a janitor for twenty-five years and is now president of a multimillion-dollar janitorial service that covers thirteen states. He is living proof that when you become the best at something—even housework!—you also receive recognition and your self-esteem improves. My favorite chapter from his book is called "What to Expect Out of Your Husband and Children." It consists of two blank pages. Nothing . . . which is exactly what you can expect in help from most family members. Although this is a humorous example, it does happen if one family member allows others to be irresponsible. It is estimated that only five percent of husbands and children do their share of housework.

7

Putting Together Your Own Success Team–It's Difficult to Soar like an Eagle When You Are Surrounded by Turkeys

Show me a man who has become a success, and I'll show you a man who had help getting there.
—C. L. Smith

When I initiated my studies in time management, I decided my most successful route would be to study every trait and attribute of people I considered successful. I was intrigued to know how they accomplished what they did, and, more important, I wanted to know why these people had been able to sell their ideas and get backing for their work, whereas other equally talented and gifted persons had not.

It wasn't long before I made an important discovery: successful people have success teams. That is to say, they have a unique kind of support system made up of family members, friends, teachers, coaches, neighbors, and people within the community who believe in them and are willing to help them progress toward their goals.

Don't get me wrong—of course the individuals I studied had talent, brains, enthusiasm, and determination. But over the years their little address books had turned into pretty extensive "Yellow Pages," so that their fingers could do the walking when they needed a resource, and they could turn their attention to other aspects of their dream or goal.

J. Willard Marriott, the corporate genius, had a wife, Allie, who worked at his side from the very beginning. She kept the books, gathered the money from the restaurants, and cooked the tamales and barbeque served in their first Hot Shoppe.

But he didn't just have Allie. They lived in Washington, D.C., and were surrounded by influential friends and family. Allie's mother had married Reed Smoot, a congressman from Utah, and the Smoots were happy to share their network of friends and allies with the Marriotts.

Barbara Sher, author of *Wishcraft*, talks about another high flyer who made his start from very modest beginnings—Jimmy Carter. She writes:

> The popular notion is that this man singlehandedly built up his family's little farm into a million-dollar business. The way he tells it, when he came home from the Armed Forces to take charge of the farm, a group of men got together with him, rolled up their sleeves, and said something like this:
>
> "OK, son, the first thing you're going to need is a certain amount of money. Here's a loan. We figure it'll take about four years till you're in a position to pay it back. Harry here has a company that'll front you the starter seeds and fertilizer. I'm not growing anything on my lower forty, and I'll let you use it so you can get started. You can use my farm machinery too, here's the key to the shed. We've got marketing contacts in every town in the state, and old Sam has the trucks. Now if there's anything else you need, you just call on us, hear? We'll be dropping by from time to time to see how you're doing."

Of course, Jimmy Carter also had a "success team" when he ran for President. It was a bigger team, more complex and organized, but it had all the characteristics of the one he started with back in Plains, Georgia.

Irving Berlin, the great songwriter, started with a success team made up of just one other individual. The story goes that while Mr. Berlin was still waiting on tables in New York's Chinatown, he thought up a terrific first line for a new song. He went to his musical neighbor named Nick and asked him to help. Together they wrote the words and music for his first big hit, "My Sweet Marie from Sunny Italy."

Recently I interviewed an ex-con who while serving time in prison developed a talent in art he had not been aware he possessed. Before we began the interview he told me he'd like publicly to thank the prison's warden, the sheriff, his family, and a whole list of people who had encouraged and supported him while he was in prison. He was grateful and acknowledged the fact that without their help he would not be where he was. Because of his success team he is recognized as one of the most outstanding artists in the Southwest.

At this point you're probably thinking, "I have no influential friends, I don't know how to make friends with such people (and besides I don't believe in making friends just to "use" them). But stop for a moment and reconsider. You probably know a lot of people who would love to be part of a success team and might even start one themselves if they were aware of how important it is to personal success. As for "using" people, you probably never think twice about asking for a cup of sugar or lending one to your next-door neighbor, do you? Well, a success team works just about the same way.

First, let's consider the various kinds of success teams that currently function in our society, and then we'll determine exactly what kind of team you'll need to accomplish your special goal.

SUCCESS TEAM A: THE FAMILY

The family is the original success unit. When it is working and functioning properly, it is one of the very best teams you can have for backing and support. It works well because the members are motivated to help each other out of love, and generally speaking everyone gets the help they need just because they're a member of the unit.

The best example I can think of in terms of a truly successful family team is the Osmond family. Everyone knows about the great success they have achieved, but few stop to realize how or why they were able to accomplish what they did. The fact is, they started out with some very specific goals—in their case it was a mutual goal shared by most of the family members. They organized their team while the children were still young, holding family councils on a regular basis. Each member was entitled to one vote and one opinion in the decision-making process. I was also interested to note that the children were not paid allowances. Instead, they pooled their financial resources and shared it according to needs. If one of them wanted $5, or even $500, and it was justifiable, he got it. For example, Wayne, one of the more introspective of the children, developed a passion for planes and flying when he was just a child. When he was only five, he began whittling model planes out of wood scraps, and at the age of fourteen he asked the family for $700 for flying lessons. Even though it was a lot of money, the family knew it was important to him and said yes. After he had earned his private and commercial ratings, he asked for a twin-engine Cessna 310 so he could start his own charter-flight business. His brothers didn't begrudge him and were happy to give him the money. Recently, I interviewed the Osmond family. The Mom and Dad give constant, sincere support and affection to all family members, who in turn display the same love and attention to one another. It was impressive and beautiful to observe.

When a family shares a mutual goal such as breaking into the music business, like the Osmonds, making a mark in politics, or even taking a trip around the world, team spirit can be extremely successful.

But there are several other family success units that can work equally well. For one thing, you don't have to be a matched set to help each other achieve your goals. I know of one family in which the parents have separate career interests and each child has a special interest; none of these individuals have any interests in common, but because of the love they share, they are able to support one another. They're organized, meeting once a week to compare notes and ask what each individual can do for the others, and they all work hard and sacrifice for one another. One very clever idea they tried was to let each family member have his or her own "perfect day" once a month. Each person did what he could to contribute to the success of that day, offering to help with chores, plan activities, or lend money to the person being honored.

Another family I know of has organized their extended family into a financial success team. Each small family unit contributes money every month to a common bank account. Then, when one member has a crisis or a special project, the cash is there to help.

The kind of team you organize your family into will depend totally on your needs. If you share a common goal, you might want a very tight, enthusiastic structure. If you are more independent, you might want to create a looser structure but to work on developing a positive, helpful attitude in each member of the group. No matter what kind of team you choose to create within your family, there are some general guidelines that can ensure your success:

1. **Organization.** In most cases, a formal organization works better in accomplishing goals than an informal one, and unfortunately many families have almost no organization at all. I encourage you to hold family councils on a regular basis, share financial matters and plans with everyone, set goals, and develop a plan of action that will allow each member to succeed.

2. **Positivity.** In a successful family organization, you seldom hear phrases like:

"No, it can't be done."

"I don't believe you have the talent to achieve such a goal."

"That would be placing too big of a burden on this family."

Rather, you hear phrases such as:

"Let's see if we can find a way."

"We may not have the financial resources now, but if we all work hard together, I bet we can find a way to raise them."

"I believe in you and have total confidence in your ability. If you fail, don't worry about it. We'll help you pick yourself up and start again."

In other words, family members believe in one another and express it on a regular basis.

3. Equal recognition. In a real family success team, everyone's needs are recognized and met. Traditionally, some families have been taught to sacrifice *all* for father, or the parents have felt they must sacrifice *all* for the children. In a real success team, everyone learns to sacrifice for the other and everyone receives benefits.

In such a success unit all individuals are treated as if they possess a special genius that deserves to be cultivated and expressed. Each member is encouraged to give one hundred percent to his own goals and one hundred percent to the others' goals.

You will note that this kind of attitude is in direct opposition to the current looking-out-for-Number-One fad. In fact, a family team structure will deepen your ties as you strive to achieve personal goals, rather than loosening them. In such a family, you learn how to bargain. For example, "I'll help you find a way to earn money for your trip to Europe if you'll give me more help with the housework," or to a husband, "I'll be happy to fix your favorite meal this week if you'll take me to that new play in town." This kind of structure can help you achieve big goals as well. Let's take a hypothetical example.

Elizabeth White, a wife and homemaker, has decided to go back to college to earn a degree. She has a child in college, one in high school, and one in junior high. Her husband works. She has made the following assessment of her needs:

> I need someone to tutor me in algebra.
> I need someone to fix breakfast on the mornings I have early classes.
> I need money for tuition and books.
> I need someone to chauffeur the youngest to junior high school.
> I need someone to help with the housework.
> I need some quiet hours for study.

Elizabeth's needs aren't overly large, and they are specific. If she were to outline them to her family in a family council, the family would then understand the specific ways they could contribute to her success. For example, the oldest child might tutor her in algebra, and the high school student could chauffeur the youngest child to school. They could all start fixing their own breakfast and pitch in with the housework. They might also initiate a money-making project to earn Elizabeth's tuition, and they could also establish a regular "quiet time" in the house during which stereos and television would be off limits.

Once again, the key to a successful family unit is to organize, analyze specific needs, and then take positive action.

SUCCESS TEAM B: INCORPORATING FRIENDS

Some goals just can't be reached with only the help of the family nucleus, in which case you need to seek outside help. Merlyn

Cundiff, a lecturer, author, world traveler, and successful businesswoman who is also one of my dearest friends and a true inspiration in my life, once approached me with a unique proposal. Her idea was to start a "people-builder organization." She presented me with a beautiful friendship ring that symbolized two hands clasped together in friendship and support. She explained the significance of her gift and the idea of becoming a people builder. She offered to help me become the best at whatever I chose to be. She would provide me with encouragement, advice, contacts, resources, but mainly support; all she asked in return was that I select one other person to whom to pass along that which I had received. I can't begin to explain what that help meant to me—not so much the benefit of her help as the conscious effort I made to be of help to someone else. The most selfish thing you can ever do with your time, energies, and talent is to help someone else achieve. You may be surprised that I would say that this is selfish. It is because you, more than anyone else, receive the biggest rewards. Giving to others helps you feel worthwhile, important, needed, and instrumental in making life better for many others. It is the truest measure of success.

You don't have to wait for someone to take you under their wing and become the recipient of their help. Initiate this idea with someone you feel has potential but is either not aware of it or is not using it. But it must be someone who wants and appreciates your help.

Barbara Sher (the previously mentioned author of *Wishcraft*) is a therapist and career counselor who began organizing Women's Success Teams a few years ago. Traveling around the country, she gave seminars and workshops to people who were anxious to achieve goals and daydreams. She helped them succeed by organizing them into teams of people who could act as brainstormers and barnstormers for one another. She describes the potential of such a group:

They [success teams] can get you a million dollars, or they can get you what you want for $5,000 or $500—or for free. They can get an introduction to Mikhail Baryshnikov. They can get you a working farm with six Holstein dairy cows. They can get you a job in a new field without having to go back to school; they can get you into school and through it without a dime. They can get you the capital and know-how to start your own business. They can get you unstuck from a low rung on the corporate ladder. They can get you married.*

Barbara Sher's idea of a success team is to formalize a practice you've probably shared with friends and acquaintances for years. For example, I have one friend who gives piano lessons to a neighbor's child in exchange for her sewing expertise. Another friend in public relations often exchanges her services with clients. Recently she gave publicity to a dress designer and received an original outfit as remuneration.

I also know of three college roommates who decided to pool their resources and talents into a success team that would allow them to achieve each one's goals and daydreams. They used the team to launch their careers, help one another find boyfriends, furnish their apartments, and take trips to Europe.

To turn this kind of an exchange into a formalized success team you need to expand and organize.

Your first consideration should be in choosing the members for your team. Open your address book, and make a list of those individuals who are:

1. **Strong in areas of unique expertise.** Smart businessmen will often hire creative geniuses even though they are difficult people to work with. They know the benefits will outweigh the discomforts. Be willing to endure the weaknesses of geniuses in exchange for the benefits you and other team members will derive.

*Barbara Sher, *Wishcraft* (New York: Viking Press, 1979), p. 112.

2. People with growth potential. Don't wait for your superiors or other great successes to pull you up. They have very little to gain from being on your team. Instead, choose from among your peers or those who stand to benefit from helping you.

Andrew Carnegie, the great philanthropist, used this important principle. As he climbed the road to success, he reportedly took forty-three young men with him. All were poor to start with, but all eventually became millionaires.

3. People who are different from yourself. Remember that you are going to ask them to do things you cannot accomplish alone. Abraham Lincoln, our sixteenth President, realized the importance of this principle when he selected his cabinet. All of the men were different from himself and different from one another.

President Franklin D. Roosevelt also understood this principle. In a letter to Henry Cabot Lodge he wrote, "You are the only man . . . who has repeatedly and in every way done for me what I could not do for myself and nobody else could do."

4. Creative. Seek out individuals who exhibit a positive approach to living. Look for people who know how to solve problems, who are dependable, and who know how to get things done. Choose people who are energetic doers! Avoid it's-not-possible, negative thinkers. They'll only ruin the enthusiasm of the group and inhibit you from accomplishing your goals.

On page 234 in your workbook section you will find a place to list potential success-team members. Once you've made your list, organize a party, invite everyone to come with their most treasured goal or daydream, and their own personal need list. I can guarantee you success if you keep in mind two important factors.

First, encourage every member to be specific in expressing his or her needs to the group. Let me give you an example. I had a writer friend who was looking for a literary agent. She had written a couple of books and had a great idea for a third one, but decided that this time she would rather have an agent market her book to a publisher. She began by checking out the writers' magazines and guides, but they had hundreds of names and she found it impossible to choose. She needed a specific person who had a great track record but would still have the time and inclination to be willing to listen to her.

As she started her search, she talked with other writer friends, complaining she needed an agent. They gave her sympathy, but no one gave her a name. Finally she decided to change her tactics. She called a successful writer who had used an agent to sell his book, and boldly asked for the name of the agent as well as any other advice he might give her for making her approach. She dialed the number he gave her, dropped the writer's name as an introduction, and began discussing her project. An alliance was formed and as a team they were able to sell her book.

Second, use your team to give you answers you can start working on tomorrow. Don't ask your success team for solutions that can help you five years from now or even five months from now. Look for a lead that will take you one step closer to your goal this week, even if it's just a tiny step. As a successful time manager, your objective is to get to your daydream by the quickest, most direct, and most personalized route.

Here is a list of some of the resources members of a success team of this nature might supply for one another:

1. **Services.** Success teams generally work best on a barter basis. Example: "I'll take care of your kids for the weekend while you and Bill go to Las Vegas, if you'll help me wallpaper my kitchen," or "I'll make a quilt for you if you'll do some macramé for me." Although members won't always expect immediate payment, you should always keep a mental "I owe you" so that when the situation arises for the other person, you'll be there. Exchanging services is especially good when you're low on cash, if you have the extra time, or when there's a particularly unique service that each of you can perform and would like to trade.

Mark Fournier's book, *How to Get on the Barter Bandwagon—Where Cash Is a Four-Letter Word* (available for $5.95 from Mark Fournier, 2808 East Dahlia, Phoenix, AZ 85032) provides many excellent examples of bartering goods and services and will give you lots of ideas you've maybe neglected in the past.

2. Introductions and connections. In her book, Barbara Sher talks about the "small world experiment" performed by psychologist Stanley Milgram, which demonstrated that if you put twenty people together and started asking them who they know, within five or six steps a bridge of personal contacts could be built to anyone in the United States. In other words, if you wanted to connect with someone who specialized in doing geneological research for people with Tanzanian heritages, or if you wanted to mate your very rare pet hyacinth macaw with another bird of equal "blue-blood" breeding, you should be able to find your answer just by getting a group of twenty people together. Someone would know someone who would know someone else who would eventually know the person you were looking for. I was a bit dubious, but to see whether this actually works, I asked one of my workshop participants to go home, select ten people from her address book, and call to ask if any of them could wangle me an introduction to Robert Redford. The next day she reported back to me two different people who could connect with Redford. One had known him during his "starving-young-actor" years and the other had worked for him at his ski resort while attending college.

To make sure this just wasn't a fluke, I asked another participant to go home, flip through her addresses and make ten calls to see whether she could find somebody who knew somebody who could get me on the "Today Show" or the "Tonight Show." The next day she reported back that she had found someone who knew Johnny Carson's tennis pro and another person who knew one of the regulars on the "Today" show.

Neither of these individuals was any kind of celebrity. They were two middle-class housewives who lived in the suburbs. So why did they have connections? For the same reason you have connections but probably aren't aware of it. Even though I never followed through in my attempt to interview Redford or appear on the "Today Show" or Johnny Carson's show, it proved we all have a great deal of information and are better connected to the big wide world than most of us realize. Generally we don't need to connect with Robert Redford or Johnny Carson so we don't make a conscious effort to think about how the task might be accomplished. But when such a question is put to you, you can come up with some amazing answers. Suddenly you remember you do have an old friend who had once mentioned she knew Robert Redford during his "struggling years," or that the fellow who taught the tennis clinic at your club last year was Johnny Carson's pro.

Dian Thomas, author of *Roughing It Easy* (New York: Warner Books, 1976) and other best-selling books about outdoor life, is an important member of my success team. As a guest on my television show she was just beginning to promote her newly published book on camping. In fact, my show was one of the first television shows she had been on. I encouraged her, telling her that her book had great potential because of its uniqueness, visual appeal, and her ability to demonstrate ideas on television. I advised her to pursue promoting it on other shows around the country. My enthusiasm was sincere, as evidenced by my scheduling her for two more appearances right away.

She followed my advice and is now one of the country's leading authorities on outdoor life, a best-selling author as well as a regular on the "Today Show."

What did I get out of encouraging her? First, I gained a dear and true friend whom I treasure. Second, when ABC's "Good Morning America," viewed by over eight million people, asked her to recommend someone else who was at ease in front of a camera and could discuss camping tips, Dian recommended me. Because of our support of each other, we both were on national

TV at the same time. Anything you do to help someone else is always a benefit to you — often in ways you can not predict.

If you put a group of ten or fifteen people together and they exhibit the important qualities mentioned earlier, they are going to have the means to solve just about any problem you can name.

3. Borrowing. Success teams made up of friends and neighbors are great when you need to borrow something, whether it's a cup of sugar, a cabin for the weekend, or a classy-looking briefcase when you go and apply for that new job. As long as you return it in good repair and take total responsibility for the item while you have it, you don't need to worry.

4. Manpower (or womanpower). Do you need a backyard fence painted? Throw a party and ask all of your friends to pitch in. Do you have an overwhelming task to accomplish, like stuffing 500 envelopes, or making 150 phone calls asking for donations to your favorite charity? Ask your success team for help. It will save you literally hundreds of hours of time and effort.

SUCCESS TEAM C: THE SUPERPOWERS OF SOCIETY

Success teams are absolutely necessary, and one of the superpowers in developing success teams is Mary Kay Ash, founder of Mary Kay Cosmetics. When I interviewed this incredible lady I realized the secret of her success was her desire to help other people. For years she had been involved in a sales program that offered little reward or incentive and neglected the needs of women. She decided to start a business that would really give other women an opportunity to become successful commensurate with their efforts: a company equal to the ambitions of women.

She formed a company based on the principal of putting

God first, family second, and career third. Each person is in business for herself, but not by herself. In order to become a top money earner you must help other people become successful. This amazing company's policy of rewarding people for helping others demonstrates the practical validity of the philosophy. As I've said before, we become rich to the extent that we enrich others.

When a consultant becomes a director at Mary Kay, she does everything possible to motivate, inspire, educate, and encourage her consultants or her recruits to be the best they are capable of. The company pays her a bonus in relation to her efforts. The individual she helps and observes becoming successful gives her a rich feeling. Mary Kay gives her a rich pocketbook. Can you imagine anything more rewarding than helping other people become successful and being paid a bonus for your efforts? This is also the way life is. Mary Kay just structured a company around the principles of prosperity.

I don't know of any company in our nation that offers more rewards, opportunity, and enrichment than this company. I loved hearing Shirley Hutton, one of the company's top national directors, who earns over $35,000 a month, tell of sitting next to a corporate vice president on a flight into Phoenix. The executive, upon learning Shirley worked at Mary Kay, said, "Oh, don't tell me you drive one of those tacky pink Cadillacs." Shirley responded with pride that indeed she did, that in her company pink was spelled f-r-e-e. Later she asked very innocently, "And what color Cadillac did your company buy you?"

Now, how many women dream of driving around in a brand new Cadillac with their name engraved on the dashboard? Few would pass up the opportunity if it were offered them, but only two percent of the thousands of consultants capable of earning a Cadillac as a reward for high-volume sales really try to obtain this goal. That's the reason it is so easy for the two percent who focus their efforts and concentrate their power. They are only competing with two percent of the population of the company.

The rest are not *really* trying. It's just like the saying, "The world steps aside for the person that knows where he is going." You're never competing with one hundred percent of the population. Only two percent really care about being successful. Don't feel outnumbered. Only a few people want the same measure of success you're striving for.

Mary Kay's autobiography, *Mary Kay*, is published by Harper & Row. I feel it is one of the most outstanding success stories of our time. It proves once again that if a person has enough energy it is possible to succeed both in raising a family and in business. Energy, faith, and enthusiasm demonstrate that a person is in time with the infinite. I believe that Mary Kay Ash is one such individual.

William James pointed out, "One of the deepest drives of human nature is the desire to be appreciated." Mary Kay gives women that feeling, and I'm told her company employs more women earning over $50,000 than any other business in our nation.

A success team made up of friends might get you an introduction to that literary agent or charitable millionaire, but if you want that individual to join your ranks with his aid and support, you've got to be prepared.

A variety of goals and daydreams requires the backing of some very key, talented, and powerful individuals. For example, if you want to run for political office, sell your songs to a record producer, borrow a million dollars to manufacture your unique invention, or train for the Olympics under a special coach, it's going to take some clout—and probably a lot of it. How do you prepare your presentation for such people? Consider these guidelines:

1. Prepare a portfolio of your project. On the first page write about your daydream, goal, or objective in vivid detail. State exactly what you want to accomplish. On following pages describe what you've already accomplished and what still has to be done. Demonstrate a winning style.

2. For yourself, prepare a list of the reasons why this person

will want to back you. Note the benefits he or she will derive from helping you achieve your goal. When you make your verbal proposal, this will give you added confidence.

3. Make an appointment with each individual. In preparation, groom yourself well. You might use this little checklist as a guide to assessing your personal preparedness for the interview:

- Do you believe in yourself? Tell yourself why.
- Do you deserve the confidence of others? List at least five specific reasons why the bank should loan you $100,000, or ABC Manufacturers should be interested in your invention.
- Think about all the bad, "failure" habits you have overcome and the good, "success" habits you have developed.
- Analyze your track record of successes. List the projects you have already completed and mentally congratulate yourself.
- Ask yourself whether you have made the commitment to do everything possible to achieve your goal or objective.

If you feel good about the answers to all of the above questions (especially the last one), then dress yourself like a winner, put on a smile, and march through that door.

4. Find out everything you can about the person you are approaching. What are his greatest motivations? His goals? His strengths and weaknesses? What does he appreciate in another individual? Do you have some of those admired qualities? This potential success-team member must want to help you. He must totally believe in you.

5. If you feel nervous about approaching and talking to the man or woman, don't be afraid to admit your feelings in a cheerful sort of way. Speaking of your own fears is often a good ice breaker, and it helps to chase them away.

6. Be natural, sincere, and honest. Be the best you can be, but be yourself. Look the individual straight in the eye, smile, and get right to the point. If you are talking to a bank officer, say, "I would like you to loan me five thousand dollars, and these are the reasons why . . . " Calvin Lehew, a friend of mine, as previously mentioned, has served on the board of directors of a bank in Tennessee and has admitted to me that individuals who dress the best they can and have an air of confidence and enthusiasm are far more likely to secure a bank loan than someone who projects low self-esteem, even if he has a lot of brains and talent. Physical impressions are often the most lasting, so make sure you take care of yourself. Learn to sell yourself in order for others to have faith in you.

7. Don't talk too much. Have an extra copy of your portfolio to leave with your contact. If his time is short, he will be able to review your proposal at a later date.

8. As you summarize your project and request, ask, "What do you think?" or "How do you like my idea?", then listen. Always express appreciation for criticism or advice.

9. If the individual turns you down, ask why. Sometimes you can correct or alleviate her negative impressions. But if you strike out, there are others you can approach.

Paula Nelson, who wrote the best-seller *The Joy of Money,* tried thirty different editors before she found someone who would publish her book. Learn from your mistakes and rejections and then keep trying. If you've done your share of the work and have truly become a person worth helping, you will find somebody who can move you toward your goal.

A friend who wanted to start a technical trade school and was turned down for financing by ten different lending institutions stated later that he was too dumb not to go on to the eleventh—where he finally got the loan.

Remember two important words, *patience* and *persistence.* Someone once said, "Everything comes to those who wait." I believe that "Everything comes to those who are prepared." A winning personality backed by positive action will not go unnoticed for long.

On page 235 of your workbook section you will find a sample

preparation profile to fill out on each important or key member of your future success team. Consider each item seriously before making your approach.

SAVING TIME THROUGH YOUR SUCCESS TEAM

In case it isn't obvious to you yet, a good success team can save you time, particularly in the journey toward your goals and objectives. In analyzing the kind of team you want to create, analyze your needs. Try and be as specific as possible. Do you need, for example, a housekeeper? A secretary? A weekend retreat? The loan of a mink? A few lessons in gourmet cooking? More time out of your schedule free from interruptions? If you can't accomplish any of these on your own, then start forming a team and get some help. I am presently working on this book in a beautiful cabin in northern Arizona owned by friends who are members of my success and support team. They volunteered its use when I mentioned I needed to get away from distractions to complete my manuscript. I look forward to the opportunity to return their help.

While we have discussed three different kinds of success teams, your needs may dictate a combination of all three, or you may need a different team for each stage in the progression toward your goal.

Remember, too, that it is as important to give help as to receive it. A friend of mine used to say, "Cast your bread upon the water and it will come back chocolate cake." When you receive help from others you save time, money, and frustration. But when you give help to someone else you get a special satisfaction in your heart realizing you have helped another individual make their dreams come true too.

So often during my seminars women will ask me what to

do about a spouse who is not supportive of their goals, ambitions, and desires. This is not an unusual situation. I always tell them about securing a support system or success team to keep their dreams alive with needed encouragement and support. It makes a big difference if there is someone who believes in you and is willing to help. Who says it has to be your spouse? Maybe he has his own needs that are so great he is simply drained at the end of the day. Do we sometimes expect too much from one person? Very often other people can be more objective in their advice to us than a spouse.

Solving Problems the Fastest, Easiest Way

Live in the answer, not in the problem.
—Author unknown

Not long ago I received a letter from a client who had taken one of my time-management seminars. The letter read as follows:

Dear Rita:

I loved your seminar! In fact, you had me believing I could conquer the world when it was over. So I went home, made a list of my daydreams, and started working on the assignments you gave us. But suddenly I started running into problems—not just one or two minor ones, but great big gigantic ones. I still believe in miracles and I'd still like to believe you can get what you want out of life, but I just don't know how to remove these roadblocks.

Can you tell me why some people can solve just about any problem that comes their way, and why others (like myself) have trouble with just the smallest roadblocks, let alone the mountains? Meanwhile it sure seems like I'm wasting a lot of time.

Rita, you taught us everything we needed to know about managing our time except what to do when a problem got in the way. Here's a list of mine. Please advise.

Yours truly,

Frustrated in Phoenix

After reading that letter and reviewing her list of problems, I started doing some hard thinking on the art of problem solving, asking myself some similar questions. From a time manager's point of view I made three important observations:

1. Everyone has to cope with problems. I don't care if you're Miss Universe and you've got a million dollars—you've still got to deal with some negative situations from time to time.

2. Daydreamers and goal seekers have more than their share of problems to deal with. In fact, anytime you try to make progress or strike out on a new path, you're going to run into difficulties. If you handle them successfully, you'll achieve your goal. If you don't you'll get stuck and probably give up.

3. Problems can consume time—and lots of it—so if you're going to be one hundred percent in control of your time and your life, you've got to learn how to be in control of your problems.

The problem is—how do you do it? How do you go from ineffective bungling to creative, effective coping? Most high schools and universities don't offer classes in problem solving, and you can't study problem solving from a private teacher as you might study piano, painting, or the saxophone. So how do we learn?

Most of us struggle through life's situations by trial and error. Sometimes we become successful problem solvers by watching and observing others, but I think there are some better ways, and I'd like to share them with you.

THE BARRIERS

First, let's consider the barriers to coping effectively. Unfortunately there are several common ones created by parents, teachers, friends, the school system, the government—by just about everyone. Then we have our own kinds of mental and emotional barriers. Let's look at some of them.

Judging Versus Generating Ideas

A lot of people prefer to judge ideas rather than generate them. Parents and teachers are some of the worst offenders. As a child you might have had a great idea for making a million dollars or solving the world's pollution problems. Yet I'll bet if you ran in and told your mom about it or wrote about it in a school paper, the adult's response was, "It can't be done." And you probably went away thinking, "Dumb me. Why did I ever get such an idea? Maybe I should just give up thinking."

And so a lot of us do give up thinking, and in doing so we lose our ability to generate good ideas. The effective problem solver, on the other hand, is full of ideas. She seldom puts limitations on her imagination and never puts limitations on her possible coping strategies.

Let's go back to the case of Paula Nelson. If you had the goal of writing a best-seller on money management and also had future plans for becoming a financial consultant on a major network show, you might assume you need a college degree—perhaps even a doctorate in the field of finance or economics. Yet Paula Nelson only went to college for six days. In other words, she found another road that would allow her to achieve her objectives—a road more suited to her specific needs and interests.

One of the keys to becoming a successful problem solver is learning how to find the solution that most perfectly meets your needs. Society often tells us we have to fit into a specific mold to achieve a goal or solve a problem. If we don't fit the mold or have access to the necessary resources we often give up. We have to break out of that mental straitjacket if we really want to take control of our problems.

Wanting Results Too Quickly

Sometimes our impatience to find a solution to our problems too quickly can actually cause us to waste time. We end up taking a simple aspirin for a heart attack, thus doing more harm than good.

Let me cite an example. I have a friend who, by her own admission, is a foodaholic. For ten years she tried every short-order crash diet on the market. She invested hundreds of dollars on so-called miracle gimmicks and treatments, and yet in the end she still hadn't solved her problem and was actually heavier than when she began her quest.

Finally she decided to get a handle on the problem for good. She closed her eyes to the magazine and newspaper ads promising immediate results and embarked on a modified food program designed to change her eating and behavior habits for life. She didn't lose weight fast—in fact it took her a whole year to reduce down to her goal, but once she was there, she had the tools and the discipline to stay there and her problem was under control.

We often choose quick, short-term solutions to big problems because we want a fast escape from the stress and anxiety that the negative situation brings. We get so unhappy and uncomfortable that we set aside our better judgment and put our energy and money into ineffective treatments. Smart problem solvers learn how to reduce the symptoms of stress and tension, thus buying time to work out the very best answer to their difficulty.

One of the best ways to reduce stress is through a regular

program of walking or jogging. Scientific studies have shown that physical exercise can actually change our mental and emotional frameworks as well as improve our bodies physically.

Another way to reduce stress is to become aware of your physical environment. In order to get creative answers to difficult problems you need plenty of quiet spaces in your day without interruption. Clutter and noise can be distracting. When I have a problem to deal with, I immediately begin by clearing my work area. I get organized. I put away unfinished projects. I put some fresh flowers in the room and put on some soft music. In such an atmosphere I feel better and can think better.

Don't Leave the World of Fantasy to Children

We live in a society that says fantasy and reflection are a waste of time and that such imaginings should be packed away with our other childhood memories. Instead of relying on good feelings and intuition, experts assert that grown-up problems should be handled with grown-up tools like reason, logic, and practicality.

This reliance on logic and linear thought is largely a product of our Western culture, but when we depend too strongly on such ways of thinking we only give our brains half a chance to come up with a workable solution.

As mentioned earlier, scientific studies have determined that the left hemisphere of the brain controls logical, mathematical, intellectual, and analytical capacities, while the right side of the brain controls the musical, artistic, emotional, and creative sides of the personality. The right side of the brain can also store vast amounts of data and impressions simultaneously, but the left side can only store and process information sequentially.

In order to make the most of your brain in problem solving you need to use both halves. This means it's okay to throw reason and logic out the window while brainstorming for ideas, because once you've got a good idea, the left side can take over and develop, cultivate, and refine it into an easy, workable solution.

The Wrong Attitude

Most of us have learned to fear problems and hide from them, rather than positively confronting and removing them. We prefer to act like Scarlett O'Hara, saying, "I'll think about it tomorrow." Unfortunately our tomorrows slip into weeks, weeks into months, and months into years.

Meanwhile confrontation with the problem gets blocked and we slide into a rut of worry and fear.

In contrast, one of the most successful problem solvers I ever studied was J. Willard Marriott, the genius businessman with the great success team. He had incredible enthusiasm for tackling the challenges standing between him and success. In fact, he even had cards printed for all of his employees to carry with them. The cards read:

1. What is the problem?
2. What is the reason for this problem?
3. What is the solution to the problem?
4. What is your solution to the problem?

Our attitudes are probably our greatest guarantee of success in solving problems because positive thinking and belief in self can sustain us through failures and hard times, even when nothing else will.

BREAKING THE BARRIERS

We can break the barriers that prevent us from being good problem solvers by becoming aware of them and by multiplying our tools and creative resources. In handling any problem I find it helpful to review the traits of those individuals who successfully remove their roadblocks. Let's consider some of them:

Going the Extra Mile in Research

When you're trying to remove a roadblock, start by finding out everything you can about the problem or situation you are dealing with. Ignorance can only lead to failure. Consider the example of Robin Cook, a Boston ophthalmologist turned author whose multiple interests (medicine, writing, painting, Egyptology, skiing, basketball, surfing, scuba diving, interior design, and gourmet cooking) enabled him to write three best-selling novels, *Coma*, *Sphinx*, and *Fever*. But before he even sat down at his typewriter to begin his first novel, he spent some six months studying more than 200 best-sellers to determine exactly what the public wanted to read. This added knowledge gave him a distinct advantage when he actually began creating his stories, and the payoff, of course, was that all three of his books made the *New York Times* best-seller list.

Seeing the Situation from Another Person's Point of View

Barbara Sher, author of *Wishcraft,* has an unique suggestion for the problem solver who doesn't have her success team on hand to help with brainstorming. She suggests picking five or six different types of individuals (real or imaginary) and then trying to imagine how they might solve your problem.

I gave this exercise to a woman who wanted to redo her living room but lacked the necessary finances to make the improvements. Stumped for ideas and resources, I asked her to imagine how the following people might solve the problem: a European princess, an interior designer, a ten-year-old child, a magazine editor, and Robert Redford. Here's what she came up with:

European princess: "Why darling, I'd simply call up one of my rich friends, plead my case, and ask them to loan me a few paintings and pieces of furniture they weren't using."

Interior Designer: "When I was redecorating a living room for a client, I'd ask whether I could barter my services for their castoffs."

Ten-year-old child: "I'd go outside and pick lots of pretty flowers and gather up lots of interesting rocks and plants and bring them inside. I'd just imagine the rest."

Magazine editor: "I'd offer free advertising space to a furniture company who would allow me to furnish my living room and take pictures of it for a special feature."

Robert Redford: "Lola and I built our house in Sundance, and I'm sure it wouldn't be that much more difficult to build some furniture."

To get into the role of another person it helps to close your eyes and picture the character in your mind. A similar technique has been suggested by psychologist Ira Progoff. He has his clients imagine a conversation with a "respected" figure in which that individual gives them advice. Here's a brief illustration: Solution seeker: "I've been writing some good songs and I'd like to peddle them to performers, but I don't know the first thing about making the approach." Kenny Rogers (as the solution seeker imagines Kenny Rogers): "Well, performers are just like anybody else and they're anxious to find good music, but they have more demands made on their time, so the timing and the way you present your song is important. If you know somebody that they know it might be helpful, and, of course, successful people like to do business with other successful people, so you've got to act that way even if you don't feel like it."

Get the idea? Of course we don't know that Kenny Rogers would actually give such advice, but just trying to reach out for new perspectives can give you ideas for solving your problems.

Expanding Awareness with Lateral Thinking

Edward DeBono, author of *New Think* (New York: Avon Books, 1971), *Lateral Thinking* (New York: Harper & Row, 1973), and *A 5-Day Course in Thinking* (New York: New American Library, 1976), is famous for his ability to solve problems using original techniques. One idea he suggests is to pick an object, any object, as long as it *isn't* related to your problem, and concentrate on that object until you can make some kind of connection.

I gave this exercise to the woman with the living-room-decorating problem, asking her to concentrate on *spoon* until she found some way to utilize the concept in her solution.

Her thinking went like this: "The spoon made me think of a spoon collection and that made me think of other kinds of collections. Suddenly I decided I wanted to feature some kind of unique collection on one of the walls in my living room. That made me remember that my husband is an amateur photographer who has taken hundreds of pictures. So I sifted through them, picked several I liked, went to a thrift store, purchased some inexpensive frames, mounted and hung them on the wall, and I'm actually quite pleased with the results. In fact I've had several compliments."

You can do the same kind of exercise by picking an "action" word and imagining what would happen if you applied that particular activity to your problem. To help you, here are several action words to consider:

develop	recall	combine	incubate
relate	adapt	expand	eliminate
compare	design	accelerate	test
commit	create	slow down	substitute
focus	change	visualize	formulate
build	recycle	clarify	generalize
simulate	organize	list	question
test	separate	record	imagine
predict	communicate	define	practice

Make Your Problem an Asset

A lot of successful people have actually found ways to turn their problems into assets. Consider Barbra Streisand, the famous singer and actress. She could have regarded her prominent nose as a defect or flaw. Instead she made it a distinctive part of the total package.

Sometimes we just have to accept roadblocks as reality. Although Barbra Streisand had the option of changing her nose, some problems are impossible to eradicate. When this happens, you have to figure out a way to build a bridge or make a detour around the situation. In other words—compensate.

The best example of someone who did this was Helen Keller. She couldn't see and she couldn't hear, and she couldn't change either of those conditions. However, she did learn to express herself through the sense of touch and thus was able to reach her goal of communicating.

Handling Reoccurring or Generic Problems

A successful problem solver will analyze whether his roadblock is a symptom of a bigger problem or is a unique situation requiring special action. If he finds the problem is generic (meaning it reoccurs frequently) he will develop a formula or principle to apply to all such negative situations— thus eliminating continuing stress and aggravation.

Recently a client complained he was running late on a project deadline and consequently was suffering tension and anxiety. After questioning him, I found that this was a continually reoccurring problem, meaning that he was always under stress and always running late on his deadlines. After brainstorming together for solutions, we came up with three practical principles that might permanently alleviate the situation:

1. He could join the six o'clock club started by Benjamin Franklin. He could make a *commitment* to get up at six every

morning, using those early morning hours to expedite deadline projects. At that hour he would not be distracted by telephone calls or other interruptions. Do you realize this gives you at least six extra hours a week?

2. He could spend a few minutes every day planning a schedule (as I've suggested in previous chapters) listing important activities in order of their priority. He could then make a *habit* of completing the most important priority first.

3. He could hire a teenager to run his errands, drop off his laundry, and do his shopping. This would free him to pursue bigger projects, and he would no longer be bogged down with details.

Many problems can be relieved using this kind of strategy. True crisis situations will, of course, require different kinds of solutions. Learn to determine your most appropriate solutions by identifying the type of problem you're faced with.

Run a Controlled Experiment

Many psychologists who help patients with problems suggest they run controlled experiments, testing out several possible alternatives and solutions before committing themselves to a permanent plan of action.

Too often we assume we've only got one chance to solve the problem; if we fail the first time, we fail forever. A successful problem solver rarely takes this attitude. Instead he approaches his work like a scientist seeking results. He keeps trying new alternatives, looking for the best solution. He never gives up.

The key to a successful experiment is control. That means you know exactly how many days, months, or years you're going to run the experiment, how much time, money, and other resources you're going to invest, and you know when it's time to stop and try another route. You set your control factors by determining how much you're willing to risk. You only risk or commit everything once the experiment has proved a success.

Controlled experiments work especially well in human relationships, work procedures, developing new habits, financial investments, and career decisions.

Role Playing

Another way to increase your chances of a successful solution is to anticipate the results of your decision by role playing. Let's say you've decided to solve your money problems by applying for a better job. Before you submit the application or set up the interview, get a friend to role-play with you. Ask him to be the personnel officer. Work the bugs out of your performance now. Your confidence and ability will increase when you make the real live presentation.

Taking Another Problem Solver to Lunch

One very successful management consultant used this technique for several years. He taught classes at a large university and often sponsored guest speakers from around the country to speak to his students. Afterwards he would take them out to lunch and usually he would work the conversation around to consulting, asking them for their opinions and experiences. He was able to incorporate much of their expertise into his own work.

When you're faced with a serious dilemma, find someone else who has overcome a similar roadblock, take them to lunch, and ask them how they achieved their success. They may be able to offer just the advice you need to achieve success.

Setting Your Imagination Free

We've already talked about the importance of imagination and using the whole brain in developing ideas for success, but I cannot stress it enough. Successful problem solvers are almost always very creative people—that is how they are able to take available resources and information and reshuffle them to find the necessary answers and solutions.

Albert Einstein gave us a perfect example of this technique when he developed his theory of relativity. He looked at the existing information on the subject, put it together in a completely different way, and bingo! he had the theory. The experiments and research to prove the validity of his work came after, not before, the idea.

An example of another very creative thinker was the great problem solver Edward Jenner. He made one of the most effective medical discoveries of all time when he shifted his attention from why people got smallpox to why dairy maids apparently did not. From that discovery he developed the cowpox vaccine, thus conquering one of the major scourges of the Western world.

Another good way to expand your creative ability is to keep a journal of your daily learnings. Not only will it get you into the habit of "learning," but by applying your newfound knowledge to old problems you'll discover new answers and solutions. You'll also have a record of knowledge to refer to for future creative endeavors. The college professor who introduced me to this idea explained that he had been able to write an entire book on interpersonal relations simply by incorporating the notes he had jotted down in his journal over the years.

A further way to expand creativity is to improve your vocabulary. New words can provide new ways of looking at situations. You can study a vocabulary book, learn one new word a day from the dictionary, or try my vocabulary secret. I keep a notecard handy. In reading and conversations, I jot down any word that is fascinating or frustrating. At the end of the day I look up the unfamiliar words in the dictionary and then list them in my Day Timer.

Play the Odds

The best problem solvers in the world learn to play the odds. In other words, they know if they construct enough theories and try enough different solutions, the odds will soon be in their favor and at some point they will achieve success.

Salesmen understand this principle and learn to be calculating in their sales approaches. One of my writer friends told me it took her nine months to get one celebrity to give her an interview and afterwards she had to query ten magazines before she found one interested editor, but because she persisted, she was successful.

It's also good to remember the example of Thomas A. Edison, the great scientist. He reportedly constructed 3,000 different theories in an attempt to create the electric light bulb, but only two proved successful. When asked what he had learned he said, "There were two thousand nine hundred ninety-eight theories that didn't work." No wonder he said genius was more perspiration than inspiration.

Be Open to Criticism

When you put a potential solution together, get a critique from others. Don't be afraid of the negative comments they might offer, because they will be criticizing the idea, not you. No solution will meet with one hundred percent acceptance from your peers. Expect this in advance. One effective way I've taught workshop participants to handle criticism is to accept the criticism with as positive an attitude as possible and then turn to that person and ask him or her to tell you something you've ever done that was right or acceptable. They will then probably stop and reflect on their answer, thus softening the negative feeling they previously had. No one is always right or wrong.

Each time someone tells you something they do not like about you, ask them to then tell you something they do like about you. Both of you will benefit. You'll have more self-esteem, and they'll be more tactful in giving criticism.

A PROBLEM-SOLVING FORMULA
THAT WORKS

Now that you understand some of the secrets of a successful problem solver, let's start solving some of your difficulties. In your workbook section you will find five pages (237 to 241) related to problem solving. On the first page write down all the problems you are currently facing (just writing them down will offer some mental relief), then select the one that seems the most difficult to deal with and proceed through the following exercises:

Step 1: Identify Your Problem

This may be more difficult than it sounds. However, it is an essential step in alleviating a negative situation. Just as a doctor cannot recommend a cure until he has properly diagnosed the problem, you cannot act with confidence until you understand the specific or complex nature of the situation.

After you have identified the condition, write it down. A good problem statement should have several parts: what is known (what information is available to you?); what is unknown (what factors are hidden from your view?); and what is sought (what goal are you trying to facilitate?).

Don't be afraid to write your problem in a variety of ways to emphasize all angles. However, after you have firmly noted the condition, rewrite it in a question form.

For example, instead of saying, "I don't have enough money for X," write, "How can I get X." You will note I left the word 'money' out of the second statement, because it is really X you want and not the money. There may be a way to get what you want even if you lack financial resources. Bartering goods or services for what you desire is an effective way to avoid the need for money.

Step 2: Study the Causes of Your Problem

Relieving the causes of the problem may be your solution, particularly if it is generic in nature. For example, you may find that too much of your money is going out in bills each month. After a careful analysis, you discover a large amount of your paycheck is being allocated to credit-card expenditures.

To solve the problem you might decide to earn more money; however, another solution might be to close your charge accounts and cut up your credit cards. Either solution might work, but one would be zeroing in on the direct cause of the problem.

Step 3: Make a List of All Available Resources

Include your talents, friends, and skills. As you do this, you will begin to determine the framework for your plan of action.

Step 4: Brainstorm for Possible Solutions

Now is the time to call up your success team (or a selected group of friends and associates who are particularly adept at creative problem solving) and invite them to a brainstorming party.

Brainstorming for answers can be simple, fun, and quite effective. Start by giving your team a description of the problem. Let them ask you questions to simplify and define the precise nature of your roadblock. Be open with them, because they can't give you a proper solution until they understand all the symptoms and factors involved.

Then let them start generating ideas. Criticism is ruled out, but freewheeling is welcomed. In fact, the wilder the ideas, the better. Quantity is also wanted, so make sure you have a pencil and paper handy.

Finally, after everyone has given their ideas, begin the refinement process. Try combining and creating, utilizing the best elements of each suggestion.

Step 5: Consider the Time Element

Before choosing your solution, ask, "What is my deadline for solving this problem?" You may have the perfect solution for raising the $5,000 you need for completing your college education, but if it's going to take longer than the time allotted, the solution will not be effective.

If you can't fit your solution to the time deadline, ask yourself, "What will happen if I don't meet this deadline?" You may find you can stretch your deadline a bit. If you need the extra time, plan for it and take it.

Step 6: Choose the Best Solution or Idea and Chart Your Plan of Action

The way you carry out this step in the problem-solving formula is crucial, because this is where a lot of good ideas fail—not because they're bad solutions, but because they're executed poorly. Your chances of success will greatly improve if you start with the end results in mind. Then visualize your succession of steps backwards. Start with the last thing you'll have to do and plan down to an activity you can do tomorrow. You'll know you're on the right track if that step opens the door to a greater success.

For example, you may have set a goal to attend law school. The question you start with is, "Can I enroll tomorrow?" If not, ask yourself why? The question may be because you haven't taken your prelaw entrance examinations, but maybe you're not even ready to take those. Maybe you really need to enroll in some refresher courses to prepare for the exam, or maybe you need to hire a tutor to help you brush up in your weak areas. Even before you do that, you may need to raise some tuition money or find a way to obtain a scholarship.

At no time should you allow your plan of action to become too complicated or overwhelming. Remember too that all great deeds are accomplished by small, steady actions—the kind of action that allows you to concentrate full energy on a task so that you can have continual success experiences.

Step 7: Act on Your Decision

Knowing the answer to your problem and doing something about it are two different challenges. Taking action is not always easy. It often involves risks. It sometimes means overcoming habits of laziness and inactivity, and sometimes you have to do things that are really distasteful to you.

In such cases I find my greatest motivation is to imagine what will happen if I don't act. You might ask yourself the same question. For example, if you don't start that diet today or if you don't go out for that exciting job interview, what will your life be like? More important, think what your life will be like if you don't solve your problem. Living in the solution is always better than living in the problem itself.

Step 8: Evaluate

Make a habit of checking your progress regularly. Ask important questions such as:

"Is this solution the real answer to my problem?"
"Am I able to carry through with the plan of action, or do I continually procrastinate?"

"Since using this plan of action, have I learned of a better method or resource to obtain success?"

If you're not meeting with success, regroup your brainstormers and try another solution. Remember that old saying, "A quitter never wins because a winner never quits." You haven't failed until you stop trying.

A FINAL WORD OF ADVICE

I suggest you keep a record of all your problems, plans of action, and your results and successes for later use. They may come in handy when a future problem crops up, but best of all you'll have a permanent record of your achievement as a successful problem solver!

9
Dealing with Frustration

You know you are on the right track when it's
uphill all the way.

—Tanner

We are often told about the hard work involved in making dreams come true, but we are rarely warned about the long periods of emotional frustration that can be a part of the experience.

Unfortunately, it has been my experience that when we involve ourselves in any kind of creative project or goal, at some point there will be a period of utter frustration. The problems seem impossible to surmount, creative insights are elusive, and resources are lacking.

The writer feels this emotion when she cannot find the proper words to express her ideas. The athlete becomes depressed when his body refuses to perform to his expectations. The student complains when she can't memorize important information or perform well on a test.

How do you handle frustration? Can you get past it?

These are tough questions to answer, and unfortunately there are no absolutes. However, a great deal of your success will depend on how well you understand your frustration and the

151

way you choose to eliminate it. In this chapter we are going to take a look at different aspects of frustration, and then we are going to examine the best way to overcome it.

DEFINING FRUSTRATION

Defined in the most general terms, frustration is simply a term used to describe the emotions we feel or experience when we can't have what we want. Specifically, there are five major areas where frustration usually develops. Let's examine each of them.

1. Lack of resources. Have you ever found yourself needing a particular resource that didn't exist?

A client who recently participated in my workshop told me that the most frustrating thing she had to deal with were her extremely small hands and feet. Her feet presented a special problem because very few shoe stores carried adult-style shoes in her size, and the few that were available were usually extremely expensive or unappealing to her. She was beginning to feel as if she might be destined to go through life wearing children's shoes.

This was a unique problem to me, so I decided to turn the workshop into a brainstorming team for a few minutes to see if we could come up with a solution.

It took the group exactly ten minutes to come up with a possible answer. They told the woman to make her own shoes. She had never considered this alternative but decided to go to the library and see if she could find anything on the subject.

It turned out that a book at the library gave specific step-by-step instructions on how to make shoes. Materials were available, and the cost would be only a fraction of what she normally had to pay at the store. She was so enthusiastic about this turn of events that she even thought about going into business for herself and making shoes for others faced with the same problem.

Have you been feeling frustrated for similar reasons? In order to remove such a block, you have two alternatives: Create or invent your own resource; or find a way to achieve your goal without it.

2. Inability to magnify full potential. Scientists tell us that we only utilize about ten percent of our natural potential, yet I continually hear clients complain about their personal resources: comments such as, "I'm not smart enough to get an A in this class," or "I guess I just wasn't cut out to make a lot of money," can often be heard in my workshops.

Do you ever make the same kind of statements? We are often impatient with the performance of our minds and bodies. We think we don't have the physical or mental capacities to achieve what we want. But in most cases I think we underestimate ourselves. We all have the capacity to achieve much more than we think we can. I think it all starts with a belief in ourselves. We have to be sold on ourselves before others will feel the same way.

If you don't feel you have the capacity to achieve, I recommend you spend one hour each day visualizing yourself as a success. It's true that one hour is a precious amount of time and you can accomplish a lot with it, but you will never make the most of your time until you think you can.

3. Leaving the comfort zone. A comfort zone is the place in our behavior where we feel most comfortable. For some people that may mean getting up at ten o'clock every morning or sitting in front of the television set all evening. I think that most people find their comfort zone is set at a level which only allows them to watch others succeed, rather than actually getting out there and doing it themselves.

Whenever we have a goal or a daydream, part of the process forces us to leave our comfort zones and create new ones. Unfortunately, we often make this move without using wisdom or good sense, thus setting ourselves up for failure instead of success.

For example, a client will often walk out of one of my workshops enthusiastic and anxious to turn her life around. In the spirit of that enthusiasm, she leaves her sedentary existence, decides to jog ten miles a day, to embark on a 500-calorie diet, and to get up at five every morning to write her first best-selling mystery novel. She also resolves to clean out all of her closets and cupboards (by next Monday), repaint the living room, and plan a special outing with her children. She has determined she will be perfect.

That enthusiasm may last for a day, a week, or maybe even a month, but then suddenly something snaps, and she is right back where she started—or worse, she has regressed.

The fact is, no one likes pain. If you hate what you are doing, sooner or later you are going to find a reason to stop. When you leave your comfort zone so drastically, you usually hate it, even if you are doing things you think you are going to enjoy.

The key to change is to improve slowly. Try giving yourself one small success experience every day. Change your routine activity by activity. You will be a lot happier and you will have a much better chance for long-term success. Adventure is to leave your comfort zone, but there are two principles of human action. First, we tend to gravitate to our comfort zone. Second, when we can't, we tend to recreate it. An example is my friend who proclaims that she likes to go camping and rough it. But later I notice her pulling out of the driveway in a $28,000 motor home. She is recreating their comfort zone. Whenever you decide on a new goal you are leaving your comfort zone.

4. **The missing link.** Sometimes you can see exactly what you want, but you just don't know how to get it. You can't find the link that will help you connect. I find this situation often applies to human relationships and employment opportunities. For example, do you remember your high school days when you wanted to date the captain of the football team or the president of the student body? You saw him every day, in class, at the assemblies, in the halls, and he was so-o-o wonderful, but you just didn't know how to make the first move. You could barely

manage a smile, let alone a hello, and in the meantime he just walked right on by without realizing you even existed. It was painful and terribly frustrating.

Or perhaps you finally found the perfect job, a job that would allow you to travel to exotic places and meet exciting people. You submitted your application, but unfortunately so did about one hundred others and you lost out in the first cut. You probably felt hurt and frustrated. It's very hard to have something you want be so close and yet so far away.

If you are experiencing this kind of frustration, there is one very good way to use your time. Spend it profitably by making yourself equal to the desired job, individual, or situation. The old saying "water meets its own level" is a truism. In the case where you want something that is highly desirable and sought after, you must make yourself number one.

Start by asking yourself the question, what am I doing wrong that I can change? You might also want to consult with the experts, or sign up for classes to increase your experience level. It is very important to obtain more information about the job or individual involved. Keep one step ahead of the game.

5. Distance between paying the price and receiving the reward.   Sometimes clients say to me, "I've been working hard, following the program that should lead to success, and the breaks still haven't come. I don't have what I want and I don't know what more I can do to improve the situation."

I recently read of a biologist who made a remarkable discovery twenty years ago in the field of plant physiology. Yet only recently were prestigious journals and textbooks willing to acknowledge his contribution and accord him the honor he deserved.

There is only one way to handle this kind of frustration. The key word is patience. Patience is an attitude of the mind. It involves faith. It's saying to yourself, "Okay, I have done the work and I've paid my dues, it's going to happen because I deserve it!"

Edna Ferber, the great American writer, said, "A story must

simmer in its own juice for months or even years before it is even ready to serve." Frustration is what you may feel during this period. But remember, it is only an emotion, not a reality, and it can be alleviated.

THE APPROACH

What should you do when you feel frustrated? Try to follow some of the suggestions given below:

1. Identify and acknowledge the feeling. Analyze it. Understand its source. On page 242 of your workbook, you can write down all of your frustrations. Try to identify and categorize each one. You will be surprised how much this simple exercise will help you to cope more effectively.

2. Realize you are not unique. Frustration is part of everyone's life.

The French painter Degas was laughed at by his contemporaries and frustrated by the lack of a market for his paintings. Michelangelo and Benvenuto Cellini released their frustrations by writing about their anxiety. They too had their moments of despair.

The bigger the goal, the bigger the frustration. Accept it as a natural part of your life.

3. Eliminate the tension from the situation. Reviewing his great accomplishments, a German physicist said, "My moments of inspiration always come unexpectedly, without effort. They never come to me when my mind is fatigued, or when I am at my working table. Rather they come when I am taking a walk in nature."

Often our goals or dreams must go through a kind of incubation period. It is like a caterpillar in a cocoon waiting to emerge as a butterfly. The cocoon may feel uncomfortable, but at the right moment in the growth cycle you will be able to shake off the situation causing the tension and achieve your goal.

If you are experiencing this kind of frustration in your life, the kind when you just don't have the answers to your questions or problems, I suggest you spend more of your time relaxing or working on other projects. You could try one of the following:

- Taking a minivacation. For example, if you live in the city, why not head for the country and enjoy some clean mountain air. Or, if you are from a rural area, spend a weekend in a large metropolitan town taking in a few cultural activities. Try an opera, jazz concert, or an ethnic restaurant.
- Spending a weekend in a plush hotel, either with your spouse or all by yourself. Don't give yourself any deadlines or pressures. Just enjoy the luxury.
- A new experience. Consider trying something you have never done before but have always wanted to do. Take a ride in a hot-air balloon, or go sight-seeing in a glass-bottom boat. Try a new craft or learn something about mechanics.

All of these suggestions may sound a bit crazy and even like a waste of time if you've got a million things to accomplish. But they can have a wonderful freeing effect on your mind. In such situations your subconscious mind or intuition can take over, thus giving you a battery recharge and a little relief from stress. When the moment of increased awareness does come, it will probably take you by surprise. Many scientists report that their inspirations have come through dreams, as they were climbing onto a bus, or even while enjoying a fast game of handball. I have a friend who says she gets her best ideas while soaking in a bubble bath. Mac Davis, the talented singer and songwriter, told me he keeps a note pad and pencil with him at all times, and that many of his songs occur to him while he is in traffic jams or driving on the freeway. For this reason, it's a good idea to think with a pencil in your hand.

Just before waking up and going to sleep are excellent times for problem solving and creativity. This is when we are in our Alpha state. Many creative people will attest to the value of having pad and pencil on your night stand because of the benefits of writing down ideas as soon as possible.

Choosing Appropriate Behaviors

In dealing with our frustrations we always have the gift of choice. We can react to the emotion like Tchaikovsky, the great composer, who tore up valuable score sheets in a fit of rage, or we can creatively work with our emotions, making all of our work a pleasant experience.

In any case, the way you choose to react during these periods of frustration will generally determine whether or not you succeed in accomplishing your goal.

Poor Use of Time

Here are some common ways of reacting to frustration that almost always results in failure. If you give in to them, you may be wasting hours, days, or even months of precious time.

1. Destroying. Many people get rid of their pent-up energy by being destructive. I can't count the number of times some of my unsuccessful dieting friends have destroyed all their efforts with one all-out binge. Similarly, many of my more creative friends have often lost valuable time when they vented their frustrations by destroying their work.

A famous southwestern artist became so frustrated with unfair tax laws that he burned many of his beautiful works of art in the Superstition Mountains while the press recorded the event. Although it brought attention to the inequities of inheritance taxes on the estate of an artist, little was done to change the law and it caused him a great deal of anguish. He realized his talent was a gift from God, and later confided he feared he would no longer be able to paint because of his actions. I've never seen much accomplished by destruction of anything. When you destroy, you must start over. Even though you reject your project, don't throw it into the fire. In a calmer moment you may be able to review the situation with greater insight.

2. Regression.   Some people give up if at first they don't succeed. They forget inspirational figures like Abraham Lincoln and Helen Keller, and they become quitters.

A friend once told me, the only real failure is when you stop trying. Many people react to frustration by totally giving up.

3. Losing faith in yourself.   Another negative reaction is to cease believing in yourself and your abilities. It's so easy to say, "I guess I'm not smart enough to pass the test," or "I just don't have it in me to be the kind of person I really want to be."

As soon as you have made that rationalization, you have a perfect excuse for failure. But once again, it's just very poor use of your time.

4. Losing faith in your society.   Tell yourself, "It's the world I live in that keeps me from achieving my goal, not me." I guarantee that as soon as you do, you will also fail. Blaming society for your failure is a cop-out. It isn't the way to succeed. If you think society has let you down, a good use of your time would be to change or improve the situation.

5. Not visualizing success.   The day you wake up and stop thinking about what great potential you might have is the day you will probably fail forever. As long as you are satisfied with being unsatisfied in this life, you probably will be. Visualization is one of the most powerful tools I know that can aid you in planning for the successful use of your time.

6. Procrastination.   Often when people are frustrated they avoid their tasks. They make excuses and try to escape. Some people choose to spend hours in front of the television when they are frustrated. Others find more destructive means such as alcohol or drugs. If you must escape, plan for it. Plan a few hours, a weekend, or even a monthlong holiday, but don't start living your life vicariously at the movies. The real world can be much more fun and satisfying than fantasy.

7. **Worry.** Many people choose to waste their time, energy, and emotion by worrying. They never take any constructive action or use their resources positively. Instead they spend their time thinking about everything that could go wrong.

If you must worry, I again suggest you plan for it. Schedule fifteen minutes a day to sit in a chair and do nothing but worry. Then take a positive antidote and throw yourself into constructive work. Remember, worry does not change a thing. It will not stop any disaster nor will it right any wrongs. It is merely wasted energy.

Positive Ways to Use Time

Although negative reactions to frustration are common among many people, there is a way of successfully coping and getting past the situation that is causing your unhappiness. Consider the following:

1. **Get rid of your energy constructively.** Instead of going on a binge or destroying your creative efforts, exercise. Certain kinds of exercise like jogging, racketball, tennis, or swimming have actually been shown to change moods for the better. One psychologist I talked with suggested that twenty minutes of intensive exercise should give you at least two hours of positive mental time. If you use those hours to your best advantage you can go a long way toward permanently removing the situation causing your stress or frustration.

2. **Work with yourself, not against your natural abilities.** The only way really to understand your mind and body and the way it performs is through experience. Most of us follow patterns. When we come to understand ourselves, we can choose programs that work within the framework of our patterns and not against them.

3. Cultivate patience. It can be done. It starts when you learn to control your mind and thoughts. It involves believing in yourself and the world around you.

We tend to lose patience when we set impossible deadlines. Instead of giving up, remove the pressure by dissolving the deadline or choosing a more flexible one. Let yourself reach your goal naturally. If you push in an unnatural way by trying to change your comfort zone too drastically, you will only fail.

4. Establish good working habits. Force yourself to produce every day. A very successful writer once explained his production method. He said, "I write down every line that comes to my head, crazy, dull, whatever. I find that if I don't it may linger and block my better works. I write as fast as I can. After a while, something happens to my brain. Some cogs start to whir, and something striking begins to appear on my sheet." He is tapping in to his subconscious or using the right side of his brain.

5. Identify the area of frustration you are currently faced with. You may have to temporarily give up one aspect of your project, but you can forge ahead in another area that will help you move toward your goals.

Always put the emphasis on successful use of your time in the here and now. Ask yourself what you can do today, this hour, or even this minute to accomplish what has to be done.

6. Seek out new sources of inspiration. If you feel stuck or in a rut, or in a situation with no way out, find someone who was faced with the same problem and who was able to move forward. This is a great way to get yourself re-psyched up. Continuous enthusiasm is one of the greatest keys you have to ensure success.

7. Get rid of the fear of failure. We are often stifled in our progress because we are so afraid of failure. We are afraid to put something on canvas, to write our first poem, or practice our first piece because we want to be perfect. The same is often true of young homemakers. I have talked to many frustrated women who are totally frightened of trying out a new recipe, making a dress, or of repainting the house because they fear failure.

When this happens, be nice to yourself. Tell yourself that the first time you try something, it doesn't have to be perfect. After all, you can always fix something else for dinner or paint the walls again. Even when you are trying for something more important, there is always another chance. When your hands and mind are busy, it's pretty hard to think of failure. It is only when you have stopped and are standing still or procrastinating, that fear becomes too overwhelming.

8. **Work with overall objectives in mind.**   Don't be afraid to expand your mind or drop an old idea for a fresh outlook. Sometimes in the writing of this book, I have noticed that I've tried to create a particular sentence and then have tried to build the paragraph around the sentence, and even the theme of the chapter around it, just because I liked that one sentence. Of course I got stuck and felt frustrated. When I remembered my overall objective was to create an informative book and not just one interesting sentence, I was able to forge ahead. Sometimes in other activities you will have to surrender an idea or a way of thinking so that the rest of your goal or objective will not suffer. When you insist on hanging on to an idea that doesn't work, you waste time.

9. **Define your frustration in a new way.**   Try looking at your frustration as though you were on a hunt for buried treasure. Or imagine yourself putting together a complicated puzzle. You may very well have all the pieces you need and simply lack the right design or focus.

10. **You are closer than you realize.**   The difference between great achievement and mediocrity is often said to be about two percent. That means two percent more study, two percent more application, two percent more interest, and two percent more effort and attention. Consistent work is the key. Add two percent more effort to everything you do.

On pages 243 through 245 you will find several exercises to help you successfully deal with frustration. Only positive use of your time can bring about a positive solution to your problems.

In successful management of your time, you must constantly change your pace. You must push, coast, and then push again. When you feel frustrated, it is generally a clear sign that it is time to change the pace of your activities.

10
Thirty Minutes till Dinner

Let's face it! Everyone is a homemaker—especially when it comes to meal preparation, which, if you're not careful, can become a dreaded daily routine. Whether you are married, single, male, or female, you must eat. And, no one can be happy eating out all of the time. If you doubt that, ask someone who is on the road a lot. (By the way, they'll jump at the chance of a home-cooked meal, so be careful!)

I was raised in the South, where meal preparation was sometimes an all-day affair. Food simmered for hours and was highly seasoned and delicious. And I'll admit I rarely cook like that any longer.

Studies show that someone working outside the home will not prepare a meal that takes longer than thirty-five minutes. I'd like to explain how I handle meal preparation and share some recipes that are easy and enjoyable. Some of them are for microwave ovens, but they can be adapted to conventional ovens.

In college I took a course on meal planning. I never dreamed

I would actually use the information in my own home. I figured it was just classroom advice. But when my schedule became more and more demanding I dug out my old textbooks and was relieved to find practical information that was effective and saved time.

Meal planning should not begin in the car when you are driving home from work. Block off some time every week or every other week in your Day Timer "To Do" list, and make out your menus with the idea that they can be rotated. (Most family menus are variations on approximately ten different menus.) If you plan your meals for a stretch of time you can make sure your family is getting the proper nutrition and variety. (See the "Menu Planner" chart on page 171.)

When my meals are written out in front of me, I can write out my shopping list, schedule my cooking time, and allow better utilization of leftovers.

An example is when I decide to cook a roast on Monday. I take it out of the freezer Sunday night, prepare it Monday morning and set it in my oven on "time bake." When I walk in the door at night I only have to prepare my salad and vegetables, which are already planned out. When the meal is finished I cut up the leftover roast in strips because I know I can make stroganoff later on in the week, and I sometimes slice some of it for sandwiches. The key is to be imaginative and to use all resources on hand.

Another advantage of meal planning is that it allows you to cook several meals at once. I basically cook two days a week, preparing enough for the entire week with the addition of fresh fruit and vegetables. That way all I have to do is warm up my meal when I get home.

The main advice I can give you is to keep meal planning simple. If you want to entertain or show off your skills, it's another story. But if you plan simple menus, you can spend more time with your family and less time cleaning up.

Involve the entire family in the kitchen. Small children love the learning experience and the responsibility, and husbands do (sometimes) enjoy cooking. This relieves you of some of the work and it can be an enjoyable way for families to spend time together.

Learn to streamline. Meals at my house are served buffet style with everyone helping themselves right from the stove. This eliminates wasting food and washing serving bowls. Plus, there's less temptation to have second helpings. The family still sits down together to enjoy each other's company. Also, before I go to bed I empty the dishwasher and set the table for breakfast at the same time.

Three hours in the kitchen will not give you precious family time, nor will it help you earn $100,000 a year. Reevaluate your priorities, look at the meals in your house, and invest in a quick-and-easy cookbook. I would like to recommend several cookbooks that will be of help to anyone attempting to manage a home and a career. Madelain Westover, Karine Eliason, and Nevada Harward have written *Make a Mix Cookery* and *More Make a Mix Cookery* (H. P. Books, P. O. Box 5367, Tucson, AZ 85703; $4.95) which show you how to make your own convenience mixes to save time and money and give you better control over the quality of the ingredients in your family's diet. *Fifteen Minute Meals*, by Emalee Chapmen (101 Publications, 1834 Mission Street, San Francisco, CA 94103; $6.95), is recommended by none other than James Beard and presents twenty suggested menus based on 150 simple, delicious, and nutritious recipes that can be prepared in fifteen minutes or less, using fresh or frozen ingredients. Two other useful cookbooks are *Recipes from Miss Daisy's* and *Miss Daisy's Entertains* (Daisy King, P. O. Box 666, Franklin, TN 37064; $6.00).

These books will be a big help if mealtime has become boring, laborious, time consuming, or frantic. You can also consult your local university agriculture extension office for still more good advice. You can be effective in this area with a little advance planning and creativity.

Since this is not a cookbook, it is not possible to provide enough quick and easy time-saving recipes, but I would like to suggest just a few that might help you feel more creative in the kitchen. Some of the following recipes were provided by Janet Emel, who teaches food classes specializing in microwave cooking. Others are my own favorites or contributions from friends.

MINUTE MENUS TO SAVE YOU HOURS!

Stir-Fried Meat and
  Vegetables
Tomatoes Stuffed with
  Spinach
Herb Bread
Caesar Salad
Cherries Jubilee

Oven Meatballs
Julienne Carrots
Noodles
Asparagus Salad
Peanut Bars

California Casserole
Green Salad Bowls
Chilled Cantaloupe
Bran Muffins
One-Two-Three Soufflé

Clam Chowder
Chicken Cordon Bleu
Janet's Green Beans
Tossed Salad
Crunchy Apple Crisp

Sherried Beef
Broccoli Soufflé
Fluffy White Rice
Hot Rolls
Pears de Menthe

Pork and Chinese Rice
Chilled Applesauce
Snow Peas
Cucumber–Green Salad
Microwave Chocolate
  Soufflé
or Chocolate-Pudding
  Mousse

Elegant Layered Meatloaf
Eggplant Patrice
Hearts of Romaine with Oil
  and Vinegar
Rye Bread
Rocky Road Brownies

Joe's Special
Fettucine
Spinach and Romaine Salad
Toasted Herb Bread
Orange Sherbert with
  Mandarin Oranges

Catalina Chicken Bake
Baked Potato
Broccoli in Butter Sauce
Tossed Salad
Spoon Rolls
Peanut Butter Cookies with
  Ice Cream

MENU PLANNER

Use this handy chart to plan a week's meals at one time, or adapt to meet your own needs.

Sunday	Monday	Tuesday	Wednesday	Thursday	Friday	Saturday
breakfast	breakfast	breakfast	breakfast	breakfast	breakfast	breakfast
lunch	lunch	lunch	lunch	lunch	lunch	lunch
dinner	dinner	dinner	dinner	dinner	dinner	dinner

RECIPES

RECIPES

BRAN MUFFINS

2   cups boiling water
2   cups bran cereal
1   cup vegetable shortening
3   cups sugar
4   eggs
1   quart buttermilk
5   cups flour
5   teaspoons baking soda
1   tablespoon salt
4   cups bran cereal
1   pound box raisins

Combine boiling water with bran cereal and set aside. Cream shortening and sugar together in large mixing bowl. Add eggs. Beat well. Add buttermilk and scalded bran cereal. Combine flour, baking soda, and salt. Combine dry ingredients with liquid mixture. Stir in remaining bran cereal and raisins. Bake in a greased muffin tin for 15 to 20 minutes at 400°. Makes 4 dozen.

NOTE: You'll love this muffin batter because it keeps in the refrigerator for a month. Only bake the number of muffins needed and refrigerate the remaining batter for future bakings. I sometimes add a sprinkle of nuts just before baking.

BROCCOLI SOUFFLÉ

> 2 *packages frozen chopped broccoli (cooked and cooled)*
> 1 *cup mushroom or chicken soup*
> 1/2 *cup mayonnaise*
> 3 *slightly beaten eggs*
> 1 *sauteed chopped onion*
> 3/4 *teaspoon salt (optional)*
>   *Cheddar cheese*

Mix all ingredients together except cheese, put in a greased baking dish, and sprinkle with cheese. Bake 30 to 40 minutes at 325°.

NOTE: The addition of 2 cups of diced cooked chicken or 1 pound browned ground beef makes this a one-dish meal.

BROCCOLI SUPREME

Try out a new broccoli recipe on your family with one of my favorites.

> 2 *10-ounce packages frozen broccoli*
> 1 *10 3/4-ounce can cream of vegetable soup*
> 1 *cup commercial sour cream*
> 4 *tablespoons Parmesan cheese*
> 2 *tablespoons butter or margarine*

Slightly thaw broccoli by placing package in pan of warm water. Place separated pieces in a 1½-quart casserole. Combine soup and sour cream; pour over broccoli. Sprinkle with cheese and dot with butter. Bake in a 350° oven for 35 minutes.

NOTE: Grated Cheddar cheese or American cheese may be substituted for Parmesan cheese.

BROWN RICE

This will be one of your favorite rice recipes. It goes well with so many main dishes and vegetables.

1/2 stick butter
1 cup rice
1 cup onions, chopped
1 10 3/4-ounce can of consomme
1 10 3/4-ounce can of beef bouillon
1 4-ounce can chopped mushrooms, drained (optional)

Melt butter in a 2-quart casserole. Add rice and mix well over medium heat until rice turns slightly golden brown. Add other ingredients and mix. Cover and bake at 350° for 1 hour. Serves 6–8.

QUICK CAESAR SALAD

4 tablespoons lemon juice
1/4 cup olive oil
1/2 teaspoon ground pepper
1 teaspoon Worcestershire sauce
1/2 teaspoon garlic powder
1/4 teaspoon salt
1 egg, beaten
1/4 cup Parmesan cheese, grated
A few finely chopped anchovies, optional
Croutons

Place all ingredients, except croutons, in a pint jar with a lid. Shake to mix and store in a refrigerator until dinner time. Pour mixture over romaine lettuce. Don't forget the croutons!

CALIFORNIA CASSEROLE

   2 *cups rice, cooked*
1/4 *teaspoon salt*
1/8 *teaspoon black pepper*
1/8 *teaspoon curry powder*
   1 *10 3/4-ounce can cream of mushroom soup*
1/2 *cup mayonnaise*
   1 *6 1/2-ounce can of tuna*
1/2 *cup almonds, chopped or slivered*
1/2 *cup olives, sliced ·*
1/4 *cup onion, grated*
1/2 *cup celery, chopped*
   1 *cup potato chips, crushed*

Grease large baking dish. Combine all ingredients except potato chips. Place mixture in refrigerator and chill overnight. Before baking, cover with crushed potato chips. Place in a 350° oven and bake 20 minutes until chips are brown and mixture bubbles.

CATALINA CHICKEN BAKE

This dish is an ideal recipe for the busy cook; I usually prepare it before going to work and then cook it when I get home from the office. It's a good way to marinate chicken, and is great to serve for company with the Brown Rice recipe and broccoli.

   2 *large chicken breasts, split into four pieces*
      Salt and pepper
   4 *tablespoons butter or margarine*
   1 *lemon cut in half*
   1 *cup Catalina dressing*

Wash chicken and remove skin. Salt and pepper chicken lightly; arrange in a 9×6-inch baking pan, skinned side up. Place 1 tablespoon butter on top of each piece. Squeeze lemon juice over chicken and pour dressing over top. Cover with foil; bake at 350° for 1 hour. Remove foil for the last 10 minutes of baking time. Serves 4.

CHERRIES JUBILEE

It is effective to make the entire dessert at the dinner table.

>   3/4 cup currant jelly
>   2 1-pound cans pitted Bing cherries, drained
>   1/2 cup brandy
> 1 1/2 quarts vanilla ice cream

In a chafing dish over direct heat, melt, stirring gently, the currant jelly. Add drained Bing cherries. Heat slowly until simmering. Pour brandy into center of fruit mixture, but do not stir. Allow brandy to heat, then light carefully with match. Spoon sauce immediately over individual portions of ice cream.

NOTE: If time permits, ice cream balls may be made up ahead of time and frozen until needed. Remove a few minutes before serving.

CHICKEN CORDON BLEU (Microwave)

> 2 whole chicken breasts, boned, skinned, and cut in half
> 4 thin slices ham
> 4 thin slices Monterey Jack cheese
>   Shake and Bake, original flavor

Pound breasts until they are as thin as possible. Place a ham slice and a slice of cheese on each. Roll like an enchilada, bringing side ends into roll. Pin remaining edge of roll with toothpicks.

Moisten the rolled breasts with a little water and roll in Shake and Bake. Cook uncovered on high power for 5 minutes. Turn breasts over and cook for 3 minutes longer. (At this point the chicken rolls may be cooled, then refrigerated or even frozen). Place chicken rolls on serving dish, set aside.

Sauce

> 2 *teaspoons flour*
> 2 *tablespoons grated onion*
> 1/2 *cup grated Monterey Jack cheese*
> 1/3 *cup milk*
> 1 *4-ounce can sliced mushrooms*

Using baking dish in which chicken was cooked, add flour to fat and drippings, or use 1 tablespoon butter and 1 teaspoon seasoned salt. Make a smooth paste from flour mixture. Add onion, cheese, and milk. Stir well. Cook uncovered for 2 to 3 minutes on high power or until thick. Stir and add drained mushrooms. Cook uncovered for 1½ minutes. Pour over chicken rolls and heat for 2 minutes or until hot. Serves 4.

CHICKEN DIVAN

> 2 *whole chicken breasts, cooked*
> 1 *10 3/4-ounce can cheese soup*
> 1/4 *cup brandy*
> 1/2 *teaspoon garlic powder*
> 1/4 *teaspoon celery salt*
> 1/4 *teaspoon crumbled basil*
> 1 *package frozen broccoli spears*
> 4 *slices of American cheese*

Skin and slice chicken. Set aside. In a medium saucepan, combine soup, brandy, garlic powder, celery salt, and basil. Heat until bubbly. Cook broccoli spears until tender but still firm. Place broccoli in a shallow baking pan. Top with sliced chicken and cheese slices. Spoon sauce over all. Bake in a preheated 375° oven for 20 minutes or until mixture is bubbly. Serves 4.

CHINESE GALAXIE

   1 7-ounce can tuna, drained
   1 can Chinese noodles
   1 10 3/4-ounce can mushroom soup
1/2 cup cashews
   1 cup celery, diced
1/2 cup onions, chopped
   1 6 1/2-ounce can mushrooms
   1 tablespoon soy sauce
   1 7-ounce can water chestnuts, sliced

Combine all ingredients in a 2-quart casserole, cover and bake for 5 to 10 minutes at 350° or until hot and bubbly. Serves 4.

CHOCOLATE PUDDING MOUSSE

1/4 cup strong coffee
1 3/4 cups light cream
   1 3-ounce package instant chocolate pudding
   1 teaspoon rum
   1 egg white

Add coffee to cream and then follow directions on back of pudding box. Add rum. Leave in mixing bowl until slightly thickened, about 5 minutes. Beat egg white until stiff, then fold into pudding. Pour into individual dessert bowls. Chill. Serves 4.

CHOCOLATE SOUFFLÉ WITH CHOCOLATE SAUCE (Microwave)

        2 squares semisweet chocolate
        3 tablespoons butter or margarine
     1/4 cup flour
     1/2 cup sugar
   1 1/4 cups milk
     1/8 teaspoon vanilla
        6 eggs, separated
        1 teaspoon cream of tartar

In a 1½-quart bowl microwave butter and chocolate at 70 percent power for 1 to 2 minutes, or until melted. Stir in flour, sugar, and milk. Microwave at high power for 3 minutes or until thick, stirring after 1½ minutes. Stir to blend and cool slightly. Add vanilla.

Separate eggs. Beat egg yokes into the thickened sauce. Beat egg whites with cream of tartar until stiff but not dry. Gently fold sauce into egg whites. Pour into 8-cup soufflé dish. Add a 2-inch collar of brown paper. (A double thickness gives a more stable collar.)

Microwave at 60 percent power for 2 minutes; then at 30 percent power for 15 minutes; then 20 percent power for 3 minutes. The top will look creamy, not dry. Serves 6. Serve with Chocolate Sauce.

Chocolate Sauce (Microwave)

        2 squares semisweet chocolate
     1/4 cup Kahlua
        1 tablespoon cream

In a 2-cup glass measurer, microwave chocolate on 70 percent power for 1 to 2 minutes until melted. Stir in cream until smooth. Stir in Kahlua. Serve over soufflé.

CLAM CHOWDER (Microwave)

2 *slices bacon*
1 *7-ounce can minced clams with liquid*
1 *large potato, peeled and cubed*
1/4 *cup minced onion*
1/2 *cup water*
1 *13-ounce can evaporated milk*
   Salt and pepper to taste
1 *tablespoon butter or margarine*

Put bacon slices into a 2-quart casserole. Cover with a piece of
paper towel. Cook for 1½ to 2 minutes on high power or until
bacon is crisp. Remove paper towel and bacon, leaving drippings
in casserole. Crumble bacon into bits and reserve. Add clams,
clam liquid, potato, onion, and ½ cup water to casserole. Cook
covered for 8 minutes or until potatoes are tender. Stir once or
twice during cooking time. Add milk, crumbled bacon, salt and
pepper to taste, and butter. Cook covered for 2 to 3 minutes,
or just until mixture comes to a boil. Let stand for 2 minutes.
Serve with crumbled saltine crackers if desired. Serves 4.

DORITO CHEESE CASSEROLE

I'm asked for this recipe often. I bet you'll like it too!

1 *10 3/4-ounce can cream of mushroom soup*
1 *cup sour cream*
1 *medium onion, chopped*
1 *7-ounce can green chili salsa*
1 *small (7-ounce) size Dorito chips*
3 *cups chicken, cooked and diced*
2 *cups grated Cheddar cheese*

Combine mushroom soup, sour cream, onion, and salsa. In a 9×13-inch pan layer half of chips, half of chicken, half of sauce, and half of cheese. Repeat for second layer, ending with cheese. Bake at 400° for 30 minutes or microwave about 10 minutes on high. Serves 6–8.

CRUNCHY APPLE CRISP (Microwave)

6 cups cooking apples, cored, peeled, and sliced
2/3 cup quick-cooking rolled oats
1/3 cup unsifted all-purpose flour
3/4 cup packed brown sugar
1/2 teaspoon nutmeg
1/2 teaspoon cinnamon
1/4 cup butter or margarine

Place apple slices in 2-quart (8×8-inch) glass baking dish. Combine remaining ingredients except butter in medium mixing bowl. Cut in butter until it is size of peas. Sprinkle evenly over apples. Microwave on high, uncovered, for 12 to 14 minutes, or until apples are tender. Serves 4–6.

EASY APPETIZERS

1 pound bacon
   Brown sugar

Cut bacon strips into thirds and let stand to room temperature. Coat each side by dipping in brown sugar. Bake on broiler pan or foil-lined rack in a slow oven (300°) for 30 to 45 minutes. Watch so they become crisp and not burned. Drain on paper towel. They will keep for a week or two if refrigerated in a closed container between layers of waxed paper. Makes approximately 54 pieces.

EASY CHEESE SOUFFLÉ

    2 *tablespoons butter*
    2 *tablespoons flour*
  1/2 *cup milk*
       Dash Tabasco sauce
  1/2 *teaspoon salt*
    4 *eggs, separated*
    2 *cups medium-sharp Cheddar cheese, grated*

Melt butter in saucepan. Add flour and mix well. Add milk and stir until smooth. Cook over low heat until thickened. Remove from heat. Separate eggs and beat egg yolks slightly. Add carefully to warm mixture and blend. Do not return to heat. Add salt, grated cheese, and Tabasco. Warmth of mixture will melt cheese. Beat egg whites until stiff. Fold into cheese mixture. Pour into baking dish. Set in shallow pan of water. Bake at 350° for 30 to 40 minutes or until browned on top. Serves 4.

EASY SWEET AND SOUR CHICKEN

Impressive enough for company!

  1 1/2–2 *pound broiler-fryer chicken, cut up, or chicken breast*
        1 *10-ounce jar apricot preserves*
        1 *package dried onion soup mix (1 7/8-ounce packet)*
        1 *8-ounce bottle Russian salad dressing*
      1/4 *cup water*

Arrange chicken skin side up in a large baking pan or dish. Combine remaining ingredients. Pour over chicken. Cover. Bake at 350° for 1½ hours or until done. Occasionally baste with sauce that is in the pan. Serves 4–6.

EGGPLANT PATRICE

1 medium eggplant
1 lemon
4 medium tomatoes, sliced
1 large green pepper, chopped
2 medium onions, chopped
  Seasoning (salt, pepper, garlic salt, sugar)
3/4 pound sharp Cheddar cheese, in 1/8-inch slices

Slice unpeeled eggplant about ¼ inch thick. Squeeze lemon over eggplant to keep it from browning. Place layer of eggplant slices in large casserole. Add a layer of sliced tomatoes. Fill spaces with a mixture of chopped green peppers and onions. Sprinkle lightly with each of the seasonings. Add a layer of cheese. Repeat layering, ending with cheese. Cover and bake at 400° until steaming (½ hour). Remove cover and reduce heat to 350°. Cook until eggplant is tender and sauce is thick and golden (½ hour). Serves 6.

FETTUCINE

1 8-ounce package thin noodles
1/4 cup melted butter
1 1/8 cup grated fresh Romano cheese
1/2 cup heavy cream, slightly whipped

Cook noodles according to package directions. Drain thoroughly. Mix butter, cheese, and cream together. Pour over noodles and mix gently. Serve immediately. Serves 4.

HERB BREAD

1/2 cup butter, softened
2 tablespoons chopped parsley
1/4 teaspoon ground coriander
1 clove garlic, crushed
1 teaspoon ginger
1/4 teaspoon celery seed
1 loaf French or Italian bread

Combine seasonings and softened butter. Cut 1 loaf of French or Italian bread lengthwise and then into 1-inch cross-cuts. Butter all available spaces. Wrap in aluminum foil and freeze or refrigerate until ready to use. To serve, bring to room temperature and heat at 400° for 10 to 15 minutes. Serves 6.

HOT CHILI DIP

2 strips bacon, cut up fine
1 large onion, chopped
2 cloves garlic or 1/4 teaspoon garlic powder
2 tablespoons Velveeta cheese
2 large tomatoes, canned or fresh
1 4-ounce can chopped green chilis

Fry bacon pieces, add chopped onions and chopped garlic, and cook until onions are transparent. Add cheese and tomatoes. Cook over low heat until cheese melts. Add chilis and mix well. Serve with tortilla chips. This is also great with crackers.

IMPOSSIBLE PEANUT BUTTER COOKIES

I never believed these would turn out so delicious—how could they work without flour and a leavening agent? Well, just try them and see for yourself. They're not only the easiest peanut butter cookies I've ever made, but also the best.

    1 cup crunchy peanut butter (you can use plain, but I prefer
    *   crunchy)*
    1 cup sugar
    1 egg

Mix ingredients and roll into balls about the size of a walnut. Place on greased cookie sheet and mash down with a fork. Bake at 350° till lightly browned. Remove from cookie sheet and allow to cool. Makes about 16 cookies.

JANET'S GREEN BEANS (Microwave)

    4 small strips of bacon
    1 small onion, chopped
    1 tablespoon water
    1/2 pound fresh green beans, cut into 1 1/2-inch lengths
    1/4 pound mushrooms, sliced

Cut bacon into quarters and combine with onion in a 1½-quart casserole dish. Cook covered with paper towel on high power for 6 minutes. Drain off half of bacon grease. Add water and green beans. Cook covered with plastic wrap or tight lid on high power for 5 minutes. Stir in mushrooms, cover again, and cook for 3 minutes on high power or until beans are tender but crisp. Season with salt and pepper if desired. Serves 4.

JOE'S SPECIAL

This can be prepared early in the morning and refrigerated or frozen and heated later.

2 *10- or 12-ounce packages frozen chopped spinach*
1 *teaspoon salt*
1 *pound lean ground beef*
1 *large onion, chopped*
1/2 *pound fresh mushrooms, sliced*
1 *cup sour cream*
1/2 *teaspoon each oregano, basil, and thyme*
1/8 *teaspoon ground nutmeg*
1 *cup each shredded Cheddar cheese and grated Parmesan cheese (I always use more)*

Place spinach in wire strainer and rinse with hot water until thawed. Press out water and set aside. Sprinkle salt in large frying pan. Sauté ground beef, adding onion and mushrooms. Cook until the liquid is almost gone. Remove from heat, stir in spinach, sour cream, seasonings, nutmeg, and ½ cup each of Cheddar and Parmesan cheese. Pour into shallow 2-quart casserole. Sprinkle remaining cheese over top. Bake uncovered at 350° for 20 minutes, or until heated thoroughly. Serves 6.

ONE-TWO-THREE SOUFFLÉ

1 *tablespoon butter*
  Granulated sugar
4 *egg whites*
  Dash salt
1 *jar (12 ounces) apricot or cherry preserves*
1/4 *cup slivered almonds*
  Powdered sugar

Preheat oven to 400°. Lightly butter inside of a 1-quart soufflé dish; then sprinkle dish with granulated sugar. In medium bowl beat egg whites, add a dash of salt and beat until foamy. Add 1 tablespoon sugar and continue beating until stiff peaks form when the beater is slowly raised.

With rubber scraper or wire whisk gently fold preserves into egg whites just until combined. Pour into soufflé dish. Sprinkle with slivered almonds. Bake for 20 minutes or until golden.

To serve, sift a little powdered sugar over the top of the soufflé. Serve with whipped cream if desired. Serves 6.

OVEN MEATBALLS

> 2 *pounds ground beef*
> 1 1/2 *cups soft bread crumbs*
> 1/2 *cup milk*
> 1/4 *cup finely chopped onion*
> 2 *eggs*
> 1 *tablespoon Worcestershire sauce*
> 1 1/2 *teaspoons salt*

Combine all ingredients, mixing lightly but thoroughly. Shape into 4 dozen small balls, about 1 inch in diameter. Place in large baking pan. Brown in moderate oven (375°) for 25 to 30 minutes. Divide meatballs into two portions. Wrap one portion in freezer wrap and freeze. Serve with Magic Barbecue sauce cubes or make Sauerbraten Meatballs or Meatballs Stroganoff. Two meals of 4 servings.

NOTE: Meatballs can be microwaved at 6 minutes per pound of hamburger, stirring balls after every 3 minutes to get the center ball to the outside of the dish for even cooking.

Magic Barbecue Sauce

Combine equal portions of grape jelly and chili sauce over medium heat until warm and well blended. Pour over meatballs and serve.

NOTE: Also good served over cut-up wieners as an appetizer.

MEATBALLS STROGANOFF

1/2 *cup chopped onion*
4 *tablespoons margarine*
2 *tablespoons flour*
1 *10 3/4-ounce can condensed beef broth*
2 *tablespoons catsup*
1/2 *recipe (24) Oven Meatballs*
1 *cup sour cream*
Hot cooked noodles

In small saucepan cook onion in butter until tender but not brown. Stir in flour. Add broth and catsup. Cook and stir until mixture bubbles. Add meatballs (frozen or unfrozen) and cover. Cook over low heat for 20 minutes, stirring occasionally. Stir in sour cream. Heat but *do not boil.* Serve over noodles. Serves 4.

SAUERBRATEN MEATBALLS

1/2 *recipe Oven Meatballs*
1/2 *cup wine vinegar*
1/2 *cup water*
1 *bay leaf*
8 *whole cloves*
6 *peppercorns, crushed*
3 *tablespoons brown sugar*
8 *gingersnaps, coarsely broken*
1/2 *cup sour cream*

Combine all ingredients except sour cream. Add to meatballs. Cook covered over very low heat for about 30 minutes. Remove meatballs and place in heated serving platter. Strain liquid and return to skillet. Stir in sour cream and pour sauce over meatballs. Serves 4.

PEANUT BARS

> *1 package (4 ounces) chocolate pudding and pie filling*
> *1 1/3 cups packaged biscuit mix*
> *1/3 cup sugar*
> *1/2 cup milk*
> *3 tablespoons oil*
> *1 egg*
> *1/2 cup peanuts*

Heat oven to 350°. Grease a 9-inch square pan. Combine pudding with biscuit mix and sugar. Add milk, egg, and oil. Mix until blended. Pour into pan. Sprinkle peanuts on top. Bake 25 to 30 minutes. Cut into 16 squares.

PEARS DE MENTHE

> *2 quarts vanilla ice cream*
> *1/4 cup green creme de menthe*
> *1 can (1 pound 14 ounces) pear halves, very well chilled*
> *1 8-ounce can chocolate syrup*

Allow ice cream to soften at room temperature. Put in a large bowl. With a rubber scraper swirl cream de menthe into soft ice cream just enough to make streaks; do not over mix. Pour ice cream into 3 or 4 ice-cube trays. Refreeze until firm, about 4 hours.

To serve.   Drain pear halves and arrange in glass serving dishes. Place a scoop of ice cream in center of each pear. Pour chocolate syrup over ice cream. Serves 8.

PORK AND CHINESE RICE

A cinch.

> 1 6-ounce box Uncle Ben's long-grain and wild rice
> 1 10 1/2-ounce can cream of mushroom soup
> 1 1/4 cups water
> 1 16-ounce can Chinese vegetables, drained
> 6–8 porkchops, trimmed
>   Black pepper
>   Garlic salt

Mix contents of box, soup, and water in flat 9×12-inch casserole. Add drained Chinese vegetables and arrange pork chops on top of casserole. Sprinkle with black pepper and garlic salt. Bake for 1½ hours at 325°. Cover if cooked longer and reduce heat. This can be prepared ahead of time and refrigerated. Veal chops or chicken pieces may be substituted. Serves 6.

POT DE CREME

This can be made a day in advance.

> 1 6-ounce package semisweet chocolate chips
> 1 teaspoon vanilla
>   Pinch of salt
> 2 tablespoons sugar
> 1 egg
> 3/4 cup milk
> 1 tablespoon brandy

Place all ingredients except milk in a blender. Heat milk just to boiling. Pour over ingredients. Cover. Blend 1 minute. Pour immediately into 6 custard cups or after-dinner coffee cups.

Chill. Serve with sweetened whipped cream flavored with brandy. Serves 6.

QUICK LEMON FREEZER DESSERT

3   *tablespoons lemon juice*
2   *teaspoons grated lemon rind*
1   *cup sugar*
1   *pint light cream*

Blend lemon juice, lemon rind, and sugar. Stir in cream slowly. Pour into champagne glasses or pretty dessert cups and freeze for 3 hours. Decorate with mint leaves and orange slices. Remove from freezer 5 to 10 minutes before serving. Serves 8.

ROCKY ROAD BROWNIES

1   *package brownie mix with nuts*
2   *tablespoons butter*
2   *ounces Baker's unsweetened chocolate*
3   *tablespoons hot water*
1   *cup powdered sugar*
2   *cups miniature marshmallows*

Make brownies as package label directs. Meanwhile, in medium saucepan over low heat stir butter, chocolate, and water until blended. Remove from heat, stir in sugar until smooth.

On removing brownies from oven immediately cover with miniature marshmallows and then dribble with chocolate icing. Let it stand until cool. Cut into 12 or 16 squares.

SHERRIED BEEF

4 pounds stew meat or chuck roast
1 package dry onion soup mix
3/4 cup sherry
1 can cream of mushroom soup

Mix together and bake at 250° for 3½ hours covered. Or you can assemble this early in the morning and cook in a crockpot on "low."

ELEGANT LAYERED MEATLOAF
(Microwave)

Meatloaf

1 1/2 pounds ground beef
2 eggs
1/2 medium onion, chopped
1/4 cup dry bread crumbs
1 tablespoon Worcestershire sauce
1 teaspoon seasoned salt

Filling

3/4 cup water
2 tablespoons butter
1/4 teaspoon thyme (optional)
2 cups dry seasoned stuffing mix

Topping

1 4-ounce can sliced mushrooms, drained and divided
1/2 medium onion, sliced and separated into rings
1 package dry brown gravy mix

Combine meatloaf ingredients and mix well. Divide into thirds. Measure water into a 1-quart measure. Add butter and thyme; microwave at high 1¼ to 1¾ minutes until boiling. Stir in stuffing mix.

To assemble loaf. Place half the mushrooms in bottom of ring mold. Dredge onions in brown gravy mix. Place on top of mushrooms. Cover with one-third of loaf mixture.

Mix remaining mushrooms into stuffing. Spoon half of stuffing over meat in ring, leaving 1-inch borders. Top with second one-third of meat mixture.

Press edges firmly to seal. Repeat with remaining stuffing and meat. Seal edges.

Microwave at high for 5 minutes. Reduce power to 50 percent. Microwave 8 to 13 minutes, rotating dish one half turn halfway through cooking time, until meat is firm and has lost its pink color. Turn out on platter to serve. Serves 6.

SPOON ROLLS

This recipe is from *Recipes from Miss Daisy.* This book contains some of the best simple yet delicious recipes I have ever run across. It can be ordered from Miss Daisy's Tearoom, P.O. Box 666, Franklin, Tennessee 37064. The price is $6. I think you'll want one after you try these rolls. They are an elegant and easy addition to any meal.

    1 *package dry yeast*
    2 *tablespoon warm water (110°)*
    2 *cups warm water (110°)*
  3/4 *cup vegetable oil*
    4 *cups self-rising flour*
  1/4 *cup sugar*
    1 *egg*

Dissolve yeast in 2 tablespoons water. Combine all remaining ingredients and add yeast mixture. Spoon into greased muffin tins. Bake for 15 to 20 minutes at 400°. The batter will keep in the refrigerator for several days so it may be made ahead of time and baked when needed. Makes 2 dozen rolls.

STIR-FRIED MEAT AND VEGETABLES

1/4 cup oil (I prefer peanut)
1/2 teaspoon fresh ginger root, minced fine (optional)
1 clove garlic, minced
1 cup of meat, chopped or sliced (your choice)
1/2 cup frozen peas, thawed
1/2 cup bamboo shoots, sliced
1/2 cup celery, sliced
1/2 cup onion, sliced
1/2 cup zucchini, sliced
1/4 cup water

Gravy Mix

1/4 cup water
1 tablespoon corn starch
1 tablespoon cooking oil
2 tablespoons soy sauce

Heat wok to 450°. Add oil. When oil begins to smoke, add ginger root and garlic. Stir-fry a few seconds, then add meat. Stir-fry meat until brown. Add all vegetables and ¼ cup water. Cover and steam 2 to 3 minutes. Add gravy mix and cook until gravy thickens. Serve immediately. Serves 4.

NOTE: Chicken or shrimp may be substituted for meat.

SWEET-SOUR CHICKEN

    1 3–4-pound chicken, cut into serving-size pieces
    1 8 1/4-ounce can crushed pineapple
    2 tablespoons cornstarch
3/4 cup sugar
1/2 cup soy sauce
1/4 cup vinegar
    1 clove garlic, minced
1/2 teaspoon ground ginger
1/4 teaspoon pepper

Place chicken pieces, skin side down, in shallow baking dish. Drain pineapple juice, reserve 2 tablespoons of the juice. Combine cornstarch, reserved pineapple juice, sugar, soy sauce, vinegar, garlic, ginger, and pepper in a large saucepan. Cook over medium heat, stirring constantly until sauce thickens and bubbles. Pour over chicken. Bake in hot oven (400°) for 30 minutes, basting several times. Turn chicken over and spread with pineapple. Spoon sauce over all. Bake 30 minutes longer or until chicken is tender. Serves 8.

TOMATOES STUFFED WITH SPINACH

    6 medium tomatoes
    6 slices bacon
    1 pound fresh spinach (or a 10-ounce package frozen
        spinach)
3/4 cup soft bread crumbs (whirl fresh bread in blender)
1/4 teaspoon each, pepper and salt
      Sour cream

Cut a thin slice off tops of tomatoes and use a grapefruit knife to cut and scoop out centers (use the tomato pulp in another dish). Turn tomatoes upside down to drain. Meanwhile cook bacon until crisp; drain, crumble, and set aside. Cook the spinach until tender in the water that clings to the leaves when you wash it, drain well, and chop. (Or cook the frozen spinach as directed, then drain well.) Combine spinach, bread crumbs, bacon and pepper. Sprinkle the inside of the tomatoes lightly with salt. Stuff the tomatoes with the spinach mixture and arrange in a greased baking pan. Bake uncovered in a 350° oven for 20 minutes, or until tomatoes are just tender but still hold their shape. To serve, top each tomato with a dollop of sour cream when you serve. Serves 6.

11

On the Road Again

Travel can be stimulating, exciting, interesting, and rewarding. Or it can be tiring, frustrating, complicated, and a nightmare. The difference is in how simple you make it.

I remember my first trip to Europe. I was very careful to streamline and coordinate my wardrobe, leaving the United States with what I thought were the bare essentials in one very large suitcase. I look back on my one-week trip and have a good laugh.

In those days I thought the necessities for travel were electric hair curlers, a blow dryer, four pairs of shoes, nine outfits (all coordinated, of course), two handbags, three belts, a cute little hat, nine changes of lingerie, a boiling unit for contacts, perfume, every cosmetic imaginable, a portable coffee maker, an iron, and so on and on and on.

I could barely lift the suitcase, and because I was in Europe on business (and pleasure), I had to change hotels every other day. I was at the point of throwing away possessions like the pioneers when they crossed the desert and exhausted their oxen. I came home with a resolution never to be so stupid again and I haven't. Sure, I wore all the clothes I took, and used most of the other items, but I could have managed with less.

Since I travel a great deal I've picked up some pointers that I feel could benefit you. Someone has said that one of the unique features of mankind is that we can learn from others' mistakes.

I keep a suitcase packed at all times. In it I have a small compact case with a set of toiletries in plastic bottles and everything in miniature—toothpaste, hair spray, and so forth. This case could possibly fit in a large purse. (Incidently, Mary Kay Cosmetics has a great travel kit bag).

When I return home I unpack and do all my laundry, and then I immediately repack the same lingerie and nightgown and replace hosiery, and I am ready to go with the addition of what I plan to wear.

I rarely check baggage. I've had it lost, damaged, and misplaced too often, even on a one-hour direct flight. By the time my baggage was located it was time for me to return home. On that occasion I told the airlines to just hold my baggage at the airport, as I would be leaving soon, and I would pick it up on my way out of town. I decided that would be the last time I would check luggage unless it was instructional material that was impossible to hand-carry.

You will find that by streamlining and condensing, you can hand-carry everything you need with a lightweight, portable suitcase (sometimes inexpensive ones are lighter in weight and preferable). If you are having a hard time streamlining, just unpack half of what you had packed and double the money you take.

Seriously, when in doubt about an item, leave it home. Less is best. The less you take the more carefree you can become. You can always rinse out a few items. You'll be surprised that you won't get tired of frequently-worn items of good quality that are chosen to match different accessories.

When I hear people talk about the amount of time they

spend packing I'm grateful that I never have to worry. It's always good to be prepared. Once, a friend who has a world-wide delivery service called and asked me to hand-deliver a letter to Prince Rainier in Monte Carlo. He knew I could be ready in five minutes and I was! When you're busy you have to be prepared.

Use travel services that can deliver your tickets and handle all arrangements. Reconfirm hotel accommodations and pay in advance if you expect to arrive late. Then, if they tell you they are sorry but there has been a mistake . . . threaten to spend the night in the lobby and give details on how you'll brush your teeth in the water fountain just prior to undressing and getting into your nightclothes. Believe me, every hotel has an extra room. If not, take over one of the offices for the night.

For obvious reasons, try whenever possible to have someone from the company or organization you are with pick you up.

If you are a female in a strange city always be cautious. If you are comfortable with sight-seeing and eating alone, fine. But don't invite trouble. I've never had a bad incident but I've never invited one either. I'm not an alarmist, but I am cautious. And occasionally it's nice to return to the room and just order room service.

Check the weather forecast before leaving. Also, call and make sure your flight is on time. Grab a raincoat or light jacket if cooler weather is forecasted. (I live in Phoenix so every town is cooler.) Besides, for air travel (who has time for anything else?), it is usually cool on an airplane, and a light jacket might come in handy.

Learn to relax and unwind during a flight, to prepare for your later responsibilities. I rarely am awake when I take off, because by then I am taking a nap or relaxing, trying to reduce the stress. I'm usually not very talkative to the person next to me, since I am utilizing this time to relax, work, or think.

Use credit cards to pay for everything. Credit card receipts save time in recordkeeping: billing problems are more easily resolved.

Since I try not to be gone longer than necessary, I sometimes fly at odd hours to get home quickly to be with my family. Therefore, sometimes I miss meals. Usually I eat peanuts and carry granola bars or fruit. Anyway, don't worry if you miss a meal. I understand that fasting eliminates toxins (whatever those are).

Combination locks on suitcases are safer than keys and less of a problem—you don't have to worry about losing the keys.

Tip reasonably. Don't undertip, because people do need to earn a living, but don't overtip. You may just be trying to buy good will. I always carry change and small bills in a pocket so I won't have to ask for change from a five-dollar bill or look through my purse.

Take along your idea file or reading material in case of a delay or a long flight. Carry a supply of stamps and stationery or postcards for letter writers and coins for the telephone.

Develop a checklist to remind you what to pack. Don't forget your sense of humor. Traveling can create stress in the most unexpected ways. Try to relax as much as possible to avoid problems with jet lag. I wear my most comfortable clothes, immediately take off my shoes, loosen anything constricting, and take a short nap as soon as possible.

I admit, at one time I really hated traveling, but now it really isn't a hassle. Just like other parts of your life—learn to keep it simple.

WORKBOOK
Exercises That Make You a Time-Management Winner

HOW I FEEL WHAT I FEEL

Every time you feel inferior or "less-than," record it on this page. List the date and the specific circumstance which caused you to feel this way.

Date	Feeling	Circumstances Triggering the Feeling

THE GREAT PROCRASTINATION LIST

What have you been procrastinating? Procrastination can cause worry which in turn leads to lowered self-esteem. On this page note everything you've been procrastinating. Your list might include such items as writing a thank-you note or making good on a promise to your child. Or it might contain larger items like completing your income-tax forms, taking the steps necessary to qualify for a job promotion, or finally confronting your boss about that raise you deserve.

_____

_____

_____

_____

_____

_____

_____

_____

_____

_____

_____

_____

FORGIVE AND FORGET

In the first section write down all of those situations you feel guilt or frustration about which simply cannot be changed. This is for those situations where you did your best, you acted on the information you had, but it didn't quite turn out the way it should have. Remember these situations are now past tense. You can't do anything more about them, so forgive yourself and put them behind you. In the next section, list all of those personal wrongs which need to be righted. If you need to make an apology, make it. If you have a debt you've been procrastinating on, pay it, and get on with your life. Wherever there is a positive action that can be taken to improve a negative situation, list it, then do it. In the third column list all of those individuals you are angry with, feeling hurt or wronged by. Try to find a way to forgive them so that you can use that energy toward constructive pursuits.

Guilt I feel over situations that cannot be changed

_____

_____

Guilt I feel because of wrongs I have failed to right

_____

_____

People I am angry with or feeling hurt or wronged by

_____

_____

POSITIVE AFFIRMATIONS

On this page, make a list of present-centered statements such as "I do first things first," or "I have terrific enthusiasm about being alive today," or "I love myself." After you write the statement, repeat it to yourself out loud, and then visualize that statement being a part of your reality this very minute. Act on it now —not tomorrow or next week, but right now. Repeat your affirmations at least once a day.

_____

_____

_____

_____

_____

_____

_____

_____

_____

_____

_____

_____

FAVORITE WAYS TO SPEND MY TIME

List your twenty favorite ways to spend time. After you have done this, consider which activities could be built into your career success.

1. _____
2. _____
3. _____
4. _____
5. _____
6. _____
7. _____
8. _____
9. _____
10. _____
11. _____
12. _____
13. _____
14. _____
15. _____
16. _____
17. _____
18. _____
19. _____
20. _____

DAYDREAMS

On this page list all of your daydreams, goals and desires. What would you like to achieve, to accomplish, to own? What new experiences would you like to have?

WHAT I NEED TO BE HAPPY

Rate this questionnaire from 1 to 5, with "5" as the most important. After you have rated the questionnaire, reread the statements and put a star by those needs which are not currently being met to your satisfaction.

NOTE: This exercise was inspired by a similar one designed by Dr. Lila Swell in her book, *Success: You Can Make it Happen* (New York: Simon & Schuster, 1976; as reprinted in *Woman's Day,* January 1977, page 149).

1. _____ I need to surround myself with beauty.
2. _____ I need to be involved in creative projects.
3. _____ I need to have a beautiful body.
4. _____ I need to own beautiful clothes.
5. _____ I need to be physically fit.
6. _____ I need to win in sports.
7. _____ I need some quiet time for myself on a daily basis to spend or waste as I see fit.
8. _____ I need fabulous possessions, such as a custom-built home, an expensive automobile, or a swimming pool.
9. _____ I need to be a collector.
10. _____ I need to sell things for profit.
11. _____ I need to be self-employed.
12. _____ I need much variety in my work.
13. _____ I need to complete projects.
14. _____ I need much approval from my peers.
15. _____ I need friends.
16. _____ I need to be number one in something.
17. _____ I need recognition or fame.
18. _____ I need to be independent.
19. _____ I need a secure, stable relationship.
20. _____ I need new relationships.
21. _____ I need to be close to people.
22. _____ I need to serve and help others grow.

My Needs *(continued)*

23. _____ I need to travel.
24. _____ I need new experiences.
25. _____ I need to be loved.
26. _____ I need to be assertive.
27. _____ I need to have power over environment.
28. _____ I need to have influence over the lives of others.
29. _____ I need to overcome faults or obstacles.
30. _____ I need to change my character or personality.
31. _____ I need to organize.
32. _____ I need to be in harmony with God.
33. _____ I need to work in a religious or service organization.
34. _____ I need to be an inventor.
35. _____ I need to possess academic degrees.
36. _____ I need to have much verbal and written communication with others.
37. _____ I need adventure.
38. _____ I need romance.
39. _____ I need to be out in nature.
40. _____ I need to have my financial affairs in order.
41. _____ I need to feel special and unique.
42. _____ I need to be spontaneous.
43. _____ I need to feel comfortable in large or small social gatherings.
44. _____ I need close family relationships.
45. _____ I need to develop new talents.
46. _____ I need to be aware of everything happening in the world.
47. _____ I need to perform for others.
48. _____ I need to lead a balanced life.
49. _____ I need to work with children.

THE PERFECT DAY

Describe your perfect day in detail. Where does it take place?
Whom are you with? What activities do you enjoy? Be specific
—what are you wearing? What do you eat? What time do you get
up in the morning? Do you work or do you play? This is a day
designed to meet all your needs.

_____

_____

_____

_____

_____

_____

_____

_____

_____

_____

_____

_____

_____

FIVE-YEAR BLUEPRINT

Where do you want to be in five years? What is your financial situation like? Describe your home, your possessions, your life-style. What kind of shape are you in? How do you dress? How do you spend your leisure time? What kind of work are you involved in? What are your major accomplishments at this time?

_____

_____

_____

_____

_____

_____

_____

_____

_____

_____

_____

_____

_____

_____

YOUR SPECIAL MISSION ON EARTH

What kind of contributions would you like to make to mankind? Do you want to improve the environment, make a cultural contribution, invent something, or right a wrong? You might begin this exercise by thinking of the changes you would like to see made and then considering the specific contribution you could make.

_____

_____

_____

_____

_____

_____

_____

_____

_____

_____

_____

_____

_____

ESTABLISHING PRIORITIES

What are your three most important lifetime goals?

1. _____

2. _____

3. _____

If you only had six months to live, what would be your major objectives?

_____

_____

_____

_____

How would you be spending time today if you could select from any of your goals or activities?

_____

_____

_____

_____

How would you live your life if you knew you could not fail?

_____

_____

_____

_____

SHORT-TERM GOAL SHEET

What is my short-term goal?

How does the achievement of this goal relate to my overall objective or daydream?

What doors will the completion of this short-term goal open?

What is my plan of action?

How long will I need to complete this short-term goal?

How shall I reward myself when it is completed?

SAMPLE SHORT-TERM GOAL SHEET

What is my short-term goal?

> To get a blueprint made of my future custom-designed home.

How does the achievement of this goal relate to my overall objective or daydream?

> It is a necessary step in the creating and building of my own custom-designed home.

What doors will the completion of my short-term goal open?

> After I know what my dream home will look like, I can begin to look for the best piece of land on which to build it.

What is my plan of action?

> 1. Consult family members to discover what each wants and expects to be included in the blue-print of this dream home. Make a list of all desired features.
> 2. Try and find pictures of the features we want in our home.
> 3. Talk with others who have designed their home. Get a recommendation for a competent architect.
> 4. Select and consult with an architect. Ask him to draw up the blueprints.

How long will I need to complete this short term goal?

> One month.

How will I reward myself when it is completed?

> I will purchase a painting I hope to hang in the den of my dream home.

FACT SHEET: THE PRICE OF MY GOAL

Financial Requirements   Educational Requirements

_____

_____

Time Requirements   Habit Requirements

_____

_____

Personality Requirements   Physical Requirements

_____

_____

Experience or Background Recommended

_____

_____

The Characteristics of My Role Models

_____

_____

Pitfalls to Avoid:

_____

_____

HOW DO YOU FEEL?

Using this chart, keep track of your physical, mental, and emotional highs and lows for one week. Within a few days you should begin to note a cycle. Learn how to use this cycle to your best advantage, planning activities most appropriate to your ability to accomplish them at a given time.

Time	Physically	Mentally	Emotionally
7:00			
8:00			
9:00			
10:00			
11:00			
12:00			
1:00			
2:00			
3:00			
4:00			
5:00			
6:00			
7:00			
8:00			
9:00			
10:00			
11:00			
12:00			

HOW MUCH TIME DO YOU WASTE?

Make a list of the nonessential activities you currently spend too much time on (i.e., watching television, visiting on the phone, shopping, etc.). After each item, keep track of the amount of time actually spent each day on each activity. Then, the following week, challenge yourself to use those hours more productively.

Activity	Mon	Tues	Wed	Thurs	Fri	Sat	Sun

USING TRANSITION TIME EFFECTIVELY

Make a list of all the tasks and activities you could accomplish in five to ten minutes. Think of this list during the day and try to make full use of small pockets of waiting time or transition time.

_____

_____

_____

_____

_____

_____

_____

_____

_____

_____

_____

_____

_____

LUNCH-HOUR TIME

List all the things you could be doing with your lunch hour (besides eating lunch). Think in terms of your long-range goals and leisure activities. Challenge yourself to do at least one of those items this week.

_____

_____

_____

_____

_____

_____

_____

_____

_____

_____

_____

_____

_____

MAKING THE BEST USE OF YOUR TIME

Make a list of the most effective ways you could be spending your time to achieve your goals. List your strengths, talents, the things you can do better than anyone else, the work that brings you the most satisfaction.

_____

_____

_____

_____

_____

_____

_____

_____

_____

_____

_____

_____

_____

DELEGATION

Make a list of all the tasks you dislike doing, feel ineffective in doing, or wish you could delegate to someone else. List the name of the individual who would be most suited for the task.

Task to Be Delegated   Individual Best Suited for the Job

_____

_____

_____

_____

_____

_____

_____

_____

_____

_____

_____

_____

_____

VISUALIZATION

Here is a quick and easy way to relax your body and mind and allow yourself positively to visualize your future success. Practice this technique every day and try some of the exercises suggested on the following page.

1. Stretch out on a bed, a couch, or the floor. Close your eyes and take three deep breaths. Many individuals find it difficult to breathe all the way down into the abdomen. They stop in the upper part of the lungs. Think of yourself as an opera singer or distance runner. Fill your lungs to their full capacity.

2. Tighten each muscle group seperately. Begin with the toes, the feet, the ankles, the calves, and so on. After you tighten each group, allow it to relax before you move to another part of your body.

3. Now take a survey of your body. Do you feel tension anywhere? If so, imagine yourself breathing deeply into that muscle group.

4. Take seven deep breaths, again trying to fill lungs. As you inhale, imagine your body being filled with white, pure air. As you exhale, imagine your body being cleansed of any impurities.

5. Count backwards 5 . . . 4 . . . 3 . . . 2 . . . 1. As you count, think of yourself sinking deeper and deeper into your subconscious.

While in this deep state of relaxation, you will be able to visualize yourself successfully achieving your future goal. Some exercises follow:

1. Think about your physical body in future daydream tense. Upon entering the Vizualization Zone (V-Zone), look at yourself closely. Observe your eyes, your smile, and the texture of your skin.

See yourself in motion—walking, standing, sitting, working. Do you move with fluidity? Are you graceful, excited, and alert? This is the physical being that will be enjoying your future goal reality. Visualize yourself as you really want to be.

2. In this exercise you will be breaking your daydream or goal down into a series of images. For example, if you dream about singing on a Las Vegas stage, your images might include the moments before you go on stage, your performance, and the reactions of your audience. In these images look closely at details. Can you feel the hot lights on your skin? Single out individuals in the crowd and observe their facial expressions. See yourself moving, listen to your voice. How do you feel in your costume?

Now enter the V-Zone. Remember the detail of each image. Try to experience each image with all of your senses. Imagine yourself touching, smelling, tasting, hearing, and seeing every aspect of the experience.

3. Before entering the V-Zone, describe your self-image on paper. Make five statements about the way you would like to visualize yourself, for example, "I am creative. I can think of solutions to difficult problems. I am comfortable with any size of group." Now enter the V-Zone and visualize the kind of image you would like to have.

4. Choose a bad attitude you currently carry toward some aspect of your life or the accomplishment of your future goals. After identifying the attitude, think of the conscious visual image it evokes and the emotions it triggers. Now choose another more positive attitude. Think of some positive mental pictures and attitudes to put with it. Enter the V-Zone and imagine yourself carrying this new attitude with the new mental pictures and emotions.

When you have completed each visualization, count to five, open your eyes, and then get to work and start making your ideas realities!

BECOMING A BETTER YOU

Make a list of the changes you want to make, bad habits you
need to overcome, skills you need to acquire in order to achieve
your goals and daydreams.

_____

_____

_____

_____

_____

_____

_____

_____

_____

_____

_____

_____

_____

_____

CHALLENGING YOURSELF

List the promises you are willing to make to yourself for one week. Rechallenge yourself each week.

Week one:

_____

_____

Week two:

_____

_____

Week three:

_____

_____

Week four:

_____

_____

Week five:

_____

_____

Week six:

_____

_____

Week seven:

_____

_____

Week eight:

_____

_____

BUG LIST

Take a tour of your house and list the things that really bug you, like the broken shutter that has never been repaired, the closet that overflows. It might also be larger structural problems, for example, not enough storage space in the kitchen, lack of play room for the children. This list will help you to pinpoint the areas you should begin to improve first.

_____

_____

_____

_____

_____

_____

_____

_____

_____

_____

_____

_____

_____

HOUSEHOLD CHORES AND TASKS I AM PROCRASTINATING ABOUT

Your procrastination list might include a few of your "bug" items, as well as those many small and large household chores you have been putting off. After you have made your list, analyze the reasons why you have put off each job. Could it be lack of equipment or supplies, or do you feel overwhelmed because the task seems too large or distasteful? Try breaking the task down into smaller parts, and then take a trip to the store to pick up all the necessary supplies.

Item   Reason for Procrastination

_____

_____

_____

_____

_____

_____

_____

_____

_____

_____

_____

_____

ENVIRONMENTAL IMPROVEMENTS

Date   What I Accomplished   How I Felt

_____

_____

_____

_____

_____

_____

_____

_____

_____

_____

_____

_____

_____

_____

POTENTIAL SUCCESS-TEAM MEMBERS

1. _____
2. _____
3. _____
4. _____
5. _____
6. _____
7. _____
8. _____
9. _____
10. _____
11. _____
12. _____
13. _____
14. _____
15. _____
16. _____

PREPARATION PROFILE

Name: _____

_____

_____

What do I know about this individual?

_____

_____

Why will this individual want to back me or work with me?

_____

_____

What negative habits have I overcome and what positive habits
have I developed?

_____

_____

The date of our interview: _____

The results of our interview:

_____

_____

If results negative, the reasons I failed to win this individual's support are:

_____

_____

How can I correct or improve my approach?

_____

_____

_____

_____

PROBLEM LIST

Make a list of all the problems you are currently facing. Beside each one, note the general attitude you have toward the problem: for example, fear of the object, procrastination, or a feeling that it is bigger than you.

_____

_____

_____

_____

_____

_____

_____

_____

_____

_____

_____

_____

DEFINING YOUR PROBLEM

State your problem in a variety of ways. Try to look at it from different angles. Is this problem a crisis or a symptom of a larger, more complex roadblock?

_____

_____

_____

_____

_____

_____

Now express your problem in a question format. Try stating your problem in a series of questions. The answers to the questions will be the solutions to your problem.

_____

_____

_____

_____

_____

_____

BRAINSTORMING

This is your brainstorming worksheet. Ask five or six friends and associates to join you in a session of brainstorming. List all possible ideas on this sheet.

_____

_____

_____

_____

_____

_____

_____

_____

_____

_____

_____

_____

_____

_____

_____

_____

SOLUTION-ACTION

State your chosen solution. List the advantages and disadvantages for your selection.

_____

_____

_____

_____

_____

_____

List the steps in your plan of action. Set a time limit for completing each step. Remember to plan backwards.

_____

_____

_____

_____

_____

_____

EVALUATION

Evaluate your solution and plan of action. Did the solution work? Were you able to act and follow through? What mistakes did you make? What are your recommendations for the future?

_____

_____

_____

_____

_____

_____

_____

_____

_____

_____

_____

_____

_____

_____

IDENTIFYING YOUR FRUSTRATIONS

Identify, categorize, and describe the frustrations you are currently feeling. What is the cause of each situation? How does it affect your work and the way you have chosen to manage your time? How have you chosen to express your emotions?

_____

_____

_____

_____

_____

_____

_____

_____

_____

_____

_____

_____

_____

_____

THE INCUBATION PERIOD

You can be sure that the insights and answers to your problems will come if you've given your mind enough information and ideas to work with. Have you thoroughly researched your problems or cause of frustration? Have you considered all possible alternatives? Take a new look at what you've put in your mind by sorting out your ideas on this paper. List everything you know about your situation. Are there any unknowns? Can you do a little more study? This may lead to the answer you are seeking.

YOUR WAY OF DEALING WITH FRUSTRATION

There are several ways to deal with frustration; some are negative, but many are positive. Use this paper to consider all the positive ways you might deal with your stressful situation.

IF YOU ARE STUCK

Often clients come to me and say, "I'm stuck. I can't go any further in the quest for my goals." I never believe them. Perhaps you are having trouble with one particular aspect, but there are still other constructive things you can do to help you move toward your goal. On this sheet, consider everything you could do *today* that would enable you to make some kind of progress.

_____

_____

_____

_____

_____

_____

_____

_____

_____

_____

_____

_____

_____

Index